Isaiah
FOR BEGINNERS

MIKE MAZZALONGO

BibleTalk.TV

BibleTalk Books
14998 E. Reno
Choctaw, OK 73020

Copyright © 2021 by Mike Mazzalongo
ISBN: 978-1-945778-92-6

Scripture quotations taken from the New American Standard Bible®, Copyright © 1960, 1962, 1963, 1968, 1971, 1972, 1973, 1975, 1977, 1995 by The Lockman Foundation Used by permission. (www.Lockman.org)

TABLE OF CONTENTS

1. THE LIFE AND TIMES OF ISAIAH	5
2. STRUCTURES AND FEATURES PART 1	15
3. STRUCTURES AND FEATURES PART 2	29
4. STRUCTURES AND FEATURES PART 3	43
5. WHEN GOOD BECOMES EVIL AND EVIL BECOMES GOOD	59
6. HERE AM I, SEND ME ANSWERING THE CALL TO MINISTRY	75
7. CHRISTMAS BEFORE CHRIST	93
8. THE SUFFERING SERVANT	103
9. THE TRUE FAST	117

1.
The Life and Times of Isaiah

To say that the Book of Isaiah is difficult to understand is an understatement. You read the book and understand the individual words but can never quite grasp the whole. At times, you're not sure if Isaiah is repeating himself or talking about someone or something new. At other times you feel that you're on solid ground as he recounts some historical event with real people in real-time, but then without warning, he relates a vision given to him by God.

Many times the literary devices used to help discern the meaning of a passage actually confuse the reader if he is not familiar with Hebrew poetry and Isaiah's style of writing. This book will try to simplify and clarify Isaiah's prophetic message for those reading him in the modern age.

We will begin with a brief introduction of Isaiah himself and follow with how his book was written.

Brief Timeline of Old Testament History

Isaiah refers to events and times before his ministry and well into the future beyond his own lifetime. Let us, therefore, review a brief timeline of Jewish history and the various books and authors who recorded it. This will help us identify some of the major events Isaiah refers to as well as pinpoint the period of this prophet's ministry.

PERIOD	TIME	MAJOR EVENTS / CHARACTERS	BOOKS
I. ANTE DELUVIAN	5000+ B.C.	Creation, Fall, Promise of Redemption, Increasing Sin, Noah, Flood	Genesis 1-8
II. POST DELUVIAN	3000 B.C.	Genealogies of Man, Idolatry (Babel)	Genesis 9-11
III. PATRIACHY	2000 B.C.	Abraham, Isaac, Jacob (12 Tribes)	Genesis 12-50, Job
VI. BONDAGE	1600 B.C.	400 years in Egypt, Moses The Passover, Exodus	Exodus 1-12
V. CONQUEST	1400 B.C.	40 years in the desert, Arrival in the Promised Land, Judges govern the 12 tribes, Samuel	Exodus 13-40, Leviticus, Numbers, Deuteronomy, Joshua, Judges, Ruth, I Samuel 1-10
VI. UNITED KINGDOM	1000 B.C.	Tribes Ruled by One King, Saul, David, Solomon	I Samuel 11-31, II Samuel, I Kings 1-11, I Chronicles, II Chronicles 1-9, Psalms, Proverbs, Song of Solomon, Ecclesiastes
VII. DIVIDED KINGDOM	800 B.C.	**Establishment of the Northern and Southern Kingdoms, Apostasy, Destruction of the Northern Kingdom, Emergence of the Prophets**	**I Kings 12-22, II Kings, II Chronicles 10-36, Isaiah, Hosea, Micah, Joel, Amos, Obadiah, Nahum, Habakkuk, Jeremiah, Zephaniah**
VII. EXILE	600 B.C.	Destruction of Jerusalem, 70 years in Babylon	Jeremiah, Daniel, Ezekiel, Lamentations
IX. RESTORATION	500 B.C.	Return of Remnant from Babylon, The End of Idolatry	Ezra, Nehemiah, Esther, Haggai, Zechariah, Malachi
X. SILENCE	400 B.C. to Jesus	Intertestamentary Period, Production of Apocryphal (Hidden) Writings	Esdras, Judith, Maccabees

Isaiah - The Man

Isaiah was the son of Amoz who is mentioned several times in connection to Isaiah but no other information is available about him. Isaiah is considered one of the major prophets along with Jeremiah, Ezekiel and Daniel. This is because of the length of their writings and not that they were somehow more important than the other prophets. Isaiah's book, however, appears first among the books of the prophets in the Old Testament canon - a position of honor since Isaiah was at times referred to as the prince of prophets.

Isaiah's name means - "The Lord Saves." As was noted in the Old Testament timeline, Isaiah lived and prophesied during the time of other Jewish prophets (Amos, Hosea and Micah).

We know that his ministry began in 740 BC because he himself mentions in Isaiah 6:1 that his visions began the year that King Uzziah died and his death is noted by secular historians. Isaiah was married and in his own writings he refers to his wife not by her given family name, but rather by the term "prophetess" (Isaiah 8:3). He may have done this because she was the wife of a prophet, or because she herself was used by God in this way, but we have no record of it.

Isaiah had two sons that were given names which signified prophetic statements made by their father.

1. **Shear-Jashub = " The Remnant return"**
   A prophetic reference to the literal and spiritual return of Judah after its destruction and exile to Babylon for 70 years.

2. **Maher-Shalal-Hash-Baz = "haste-spoil-speed-prey"**
   This name implied the eventual attack of the Assyrians on the Northern kingdom of Israel and its neighbor Syria. Assyria was anxious to attack, destroy and pillage all of its enemies.

It is interesting to note that the Bible mentions various details of the marriages of several of the prophets, for example:

- Jeremiah was celibate (Jeremiah 16:2)

- Hosea's wife was unfaithful (Hosea 1:2)

- Ezekiel's wife died suddenly but he was not allowed to mourn her (Ezekiel 24:16-18).

- Isaiah's wife collaborated with him in naming their sons with names reflecting prophecy concerning Israel and Judah.

Isaiah probably spent most of his life in Jerusalem and judging by the quality of his writing and his access to the royal court of successive Kings (Uzziah, Jotham, Ahaz and Hezekiah) scholars believe that he was a well-educated, wealthy aristocrat or perhaps part of a priestly family.

Even though it seems that Isaiah had a high position in the society of his time, he was very much aware of the plight of the poor, the excesses of the rich and the injustices visited on the common people by those in power as well as the immorality and unfaithfulness that existed at every level of society both rich and poor.

Despite the advantages of education, wealth and access to the royal court, as God's prophet, and very much like the more common social justice prophets who were his contemporaries (Amos, Hosea, Micah), Isaiah spoke out powerfully. Not only did he speak truth to power, he did so with a beautiful, complex and majestic style of writing.

Isaiah's bold and fearless pronouncement of God's word is what probably led to his death at the hands of Manasseh, who Jewish tradition says had the prophet executed by having him sawed in two.

> They were stoned, they were sawn in two, they were tempted, they were put to death with the sword; they went about in sheepskins, in goatskins, being destitute, afflicted, ill-treated.
> - Hebrews 11:37

Isaiah - Times

Isaiah wrote during a stormy period, marking the expansion of the Assyrian empire and the decline of Israel. Under King Tiglath-Pileser III (reigned 745-727 BC) the Assyrians swept westward into Aram (Syria) and into Canaan where the Northern Kingdom of Israel was located. They then continued downwards into Israel. In response, the Kings of Aram and Israel tried to pressure King Ahaz of Judah (Southern kingdom) into joining their alliance against Assyria.

Instead of joining this alliance, Ahaz chose to ask Tiglath-Pileser for help against Israel and Aram. Today, we call that a "double-cross". Isaiah condemned this decision (Isaiah 7).

Assyria did help Judah by conquering and deporting the Northern Kingdom but this left the Southern Kingdom even more vulnerable and exposed to attack from the North. Following its desire for complete domination of the region, in 701 King Sennacherib of Assyria threatened Jerusalem itself (Isaiah 36:1-ff).

The godly King Hezekiah prayed earnestly and Isaiah prophesied that God would force the Assyrians to withdraw, and they did (Isaiah 37:6-7). Nevertheless, Isaiah warned that because of her sins, Judah would be defeated and brought into captivity by the Babylonians (the nation that defeated the Assyrians and took their place as the superpower of that era).

Although the fall of Jerusalem would not take place until 586 BC (more than a century into the future), Isaiah's prophecy accurately foretold:

1. The destruction of Judah
2. The captivity of the people in a foreign land
3. The eventual restoration of the people from their captivity and return to Jerusalem

Isaiah also predicted the rise of Cyrus, who would unite the Medes and the Persians, and these under Cyrus would conquer the Babylonians in 539 BC (Isaiah 41).

The decree of Cyrus in 538 B.C. would eventually allow the Jews to return home to rebuild their city, wall and temple. In his prophecy, Isaiah claimed that this deliverance would prefigure another deliverance, this time from sin, which would take place even further into the future.

Isaiah's many visions and prophecies spoke of people and events in the present, near future and distant future - all of which make him one of the most dynamic prophets in the Bible.

2. Structures and Features
Part 1

So far we have noted that the prophet Isaiah lived in Jerusalem between the 8th and 7th century before Christ. He was a contemporary of several Kings and he prophesied during the reigns of Jotham, Ahaz and Hezekiah. The main subject of his prophecies were warnings to the rulers both of the Northern Kingdom (Israel) and the Southern Kingdom (Judah) concerning their conduct, faithfulness to God and various relationships with foreign powers. His prophecies included:

A. Denouncing their alliances with pagan nations to secure military protection instead of trusting God for safety.

B. Warning them of impending attacks and destruction.

C. Denouncing surrounding nations for their worship of pagan gods and announcing the judgment of God on them.

D. Prophesied the restoration of the southern kingdom after its defeat and exile.

E. Articulated the form, method and the results of God's promised salvation in the future.

    1. Form - A Man

    2. Method - Vicarious atonement

    3. Results - Regeneration

These prophecies were not only given once but were repeated at different times throughout his book using various words and literary devices.

In this chapter, we will begin to examine the way that Isaiah wrote and how he put his book together. Understanding this will help us understand what, exactly, the prophet was communicating.

Structure of Book of Isaiah

Isaiah's prophecies and teachings are presented using five main topics. These consist of the following:

1. The Messianic hope
2. The Motif (pattern or concept) of the City (Jerusalem).
3. The Holy One of Israel
4. The faith response of the Jewish people throughout their history
5. Special literary and structural features of Isaiah's writings.

The book of Isaiah would be a lot easier to understand and follow if the prophet had taken each of these topics/themes/devices and written a chapter or two about each one in successive order (roman numeral I, point A, subpoint b, etc.).

However, Isaiah wrote with the eastern mindset of a Jewish prophet and poet. His five topics/themes, therefore, are seen as five individual strands that are carefully and artfully braided together, each repeatedly overlapping the other to tell a single story.

If you are unfamiliar with the individual strands you cannot tell when and where one theme/topic ends and another begins nor can you understand the message as a whole. In other words, you understand some of the words, but can't follow the storyline to understand the message itself.

Knowing the themes and features of the writing helps the reader know who and what the prophet is talking about in different parts of his book. Let's examine the five strands.

The 5 Strands

1. The Messianic Hope

The Jews from the time of Moses (Deuteronomy 18:15) had been promised a Savior but until Isaiah, the form and the purpose of this "Messiah" had not yet been clearly defined. We have references to Him in the book of Job for example (Job 19:25-27) and in the Psalms (Psalm 110:1) but Isaiah is the prophet that most clearly defines Him along with the way He was to save His people.

Isaiah provides us with three portraits of the Messianic hope in this strand.

1. The Messiah as a King
   - chapters 1-37
2. The Messiah as a Servant
   - chapters 38-55
3. The Messiah as an Anointed Conqueror
   - chapters 56-66

Although separate and distinct as portraits, all three share similar features indicating that they are all meant to be facets of a single Messianic personage. For example, let's say you name three animals - lion, bear and eagle. However, in describing each one you use words like fierce, powerful, cunning and carnivorous. All things that are true about each creature and serve to unify them rather than to distinguish them. Disparate animals described with attributes common to all.

So, in like fashion, in Isaiah's descriptions of the Messianic hope as (King, Servant, Conqueror) each one of these has the following similar traits:

A. Each is endowed with the Spirit and the Word of God.

> "As for Me, this is My covenant with them," says the Lord: "My Spirit which is upon you, and My words which I have put in your mouth shall not depart from your mouth, nor from the mouth of your offspring, nor from the mouth of your offspring's offspring," says the Lord, "from now and forever."
> - Isaiah 59:21

B. Each is imbued with righteousness as a natural state.

> His grave was assigned with wicked men,
> Yet He was with a rich man in His death,
> Because He had done no violence,

> Nor was there any deceit in His mouth.
> - Isaiah 53:9

C. The King, Servant, Conqueror are each seen as descendants of David fulfilling promises made through him.

> ⁶ For a child will be born to us, a son will be given to us;
> And the government will rest on His shoulders;
> And His name will be called Wonderful Counselor, Mighty God,
> Eternal Father, Prince of Peace.
> ⁷ There will be no end to the increase of His government or of peace,
> On the throne of David and over his kingdom,
> To establish it and to uphold it with justice and righteousness
> From then on and forevermore.
> The zeal of the Lord of hosts will accomplish this.
> - Isaiah 9:6-7

D. Each brings the Messianic hope, in each of its forms, to both Jews and Gentiles.

> ¹ The word which Isaiah the son of Amoz saw concerning Judah and Jerusalem.
> ² Now it will come about that
> In the last days
> The mountain of the house of the Lord
> Will be established as the chief of the mountains,
> And will be raised above the hills;

> And all the nations will stream to it.
> ³ And many peoples will come and say,
> "Come, let us go up to the mountain of the Lord,
> To the house of the God of Jacob;
> That He may teach us concerning His ways
> And that we may walk in His paths."
> For the law will go forth from Zion
> And the word of the Lord from Jerusalem.
> - Isaiah 2:1-3

E. Each is presented from a dual nature (God/Man) perspective.

1. King - Born in David's line - 11:1

- Man: The root from which David, himself, springs - 11:10
- God: This King, however, will be called Mighty God - 9:6

2. Servant - Possess a human ancestry and appearance

> For He grew up before Him like a tender shoot,
> And like a root out of parched ground;
> He has no stately form or majesty
> That we should look upon Him,
> Nor appearance that we should be attracted to Him.
> - Isaiah 53:2

He also was the Lord Himself appearing with salvation - 52:10; 53:1.

3. Anointed Conqueror -
The God/Man combination as Savior

> [15b] Now the Lord saw,
> And it was displeasing in His sight that there was no justice.
> [16] And He saw that there was no man,
> And was astonished that there was no one to intercede;
> Then His own arm brought salvation to Him,
> And His righteousness upheld Him.
> [17] He put on righteousness like a breastplate,
> And a helmet of salvation on His head;
> And He put on garments of vengeance for clothing
> And wrapped Himself with zeal as a mantle.
> [18] According to their deeds, so He will repay,
> Wrath to His adversaries, recompense to His enemies;
> To the coastlands He will make recompense.
> [19] So they will fear the name of the Lord from the west
> And His glory from the rising of the sun,
> For He will come like a rushing stream
> Which the wind of the Lord drives.
> [20] "A Redeemer will come to Zion,
> And to those who turn from transgression in Jacob," declares the Lord.
> - Isaiah 59:15b-20

And so, in this first strand (Messianic hope) Isaiah (through the power of the Spirit) creates three portraits of the coming Messiah with each portrait providing particular information about this person.

- A. His royal position of authority as (king)
- B. His human character as a man with a mission (servant)
- C. His ultimate victory over death as the anointed (conqueror)

The unified vision that the prophet Isaiah presents is that of a person who is a descendant of David, full of the Spirit and Word of God, and fully righteous who will ultimately succeed in bringing salvation to both Jews and Gentiles. This King and conqueror will do this because He is the chosen Servant sent by God.

The next topic/strand that Isaiah addresses is referred to as:

2. The Motif (pattern/concept) of the City (Jerusalem)

In the writings of Isaiah, the city of Jerusalem plays an important part in the outworking of God's plan.

A. History

The city is first introduced in Genesis 14:18 through Melchizedek who was described as the King of Salem (later to become Jerusalem) and his royal Priesthood was recognized by Abraham, who paid tithes to this priestly king. David captured this ancient city and made it the capital as well as the political and religious center of his Kingdom since the Temple and the royal palace were both eventually located there.

B. Significance of the city in Isaiah

Isaiah uses Jerusalem as a character and metaphor for the Jewish people and nation (first mentioned in Isaiah 1:1). The word metaphor is a word used to symbolize something else. He also uses the city as a metaphor for God's people all over the world, not just cultural Jews, those living in Jerusalem or living in the country of Israel.

For example, if you remember after the terrorist attack on New York City (9/11). After 9/11 people around the world said, "We are New York" as a way of expressing solidarity and sympathy with the people of New York and America itself. In this sense, all Christians can say, "We are Jerusalem" putting forth the idea that we are God's people. This was Isaiah's use of the city of Jerusalem metaphor. It was also used to establish the notion that what happened to the City happened to the people and nation as well as the spiritual nation itself.

C. Isaiah uses four interchangeable terms when he's talking about the City.

1. Jerusalem
2. Zion (another word for Jerusalem or holy place)
3. Mount/Mountain
4. City

D. He writes various themes with the city as the central object or figure.

For example:

1. Divine judgment on the city
2. Preservation/restoration of the city
3. Security of the city
4. The security one has who dwells in the city
5. The centrality of the city in God's thought and plan
6. The eschatological vision of the city at the end times

    o Isaiah's view of heaven was God seated as King at the center of the city reigning over the entire universe filled with righteousness and peace.

To summarize, therefore, the city of Jerusalem is used by Isaiah as a metaphor for:

A. The Jewish nation - his present time

B. All of God's people in the world - future time

C. The fulfillment and the establishment of God's heavenly kingdom - at the end of time

In this section, we've examined two of the five themes/topics/strands which Isaiah will use to present his prophecies and teachings.

1. **The Messianic hope** seen as:

- King - chapters 1-37
- A Servant - chapters 38-55
- An Anointed Conqueror - chapters 56-66

2. The Motif of the city

This is where Isaiah explores:

- The history of Jerusalem
- The significance of the city (representing the people now and in the future)
- The terms by which it is referred to - Jerusalem, Zion, Mount, City.
- He examines the city from various perspectives - judgment, restoration, etc.

- He uses the city as a metaphor for the present, near future and end times.

In the next chapter we will review the third and fourth themes or strands that Isaiah uses:

    3. The Holy One of Israel

    4. The faith response of the Jewish people throughout history

3. Structures and Features
Part 2

In building a house the first elements to go in are the foundation and the frame of the building, these give you an idea of what the finished structure will be like (a home, commercial building, barn, etc.). This is what we've been doing with our introductory material on Isaiah - seeing how the prophet put his book together. Knowing this will help us understand Isaiah's overall message.

Briefly, then, I've shown you that:

- A. Isaiah's prophecies were made during a period in the 8-7th century B.C. at which time God's people were divided with the Kingdom of Israel located in the north and the Kingdom of Judah in the south.
- B. He was a contemporary of the prophets Amos, Hosea and Micah.
- C. He prophesied during the reigns of Uzziah, Jotham, Ahaz and Hezekiah, and was based in Jerusalem.
- D. According to Jewish tradition, he died at the hands of King Manasseh who had him sawed in two (Hebrews 11:37).
- E. His teachings are contained in 5 main topics/themes which are interwoven to form one narrative (like braiding 5 different strands into one). The 5 topics are:
    1. The Messianic hope
    2. The motif/pattern of the City (Jerusalem)
    3. The Holy One of Israel
    4. The faith response of the Jewish people
    5. The special literary features of Isaiah's writing

In the previous chapter, we reviewed the first two of these five strands.

1. **Messianic Hope** - seen in three types or images: the King, Servant and Conqueror.

2. **The Pattern of the City** - Jerusalem is used as a metaphor for God's people during the time of Isaiah, in the future, and at the "end time."

In this chapter we will continue examining the next two topics Isaiah uses - The Holy One of Israel and the faith response of the Jewish people.

The Holy One of Israel

Isaiah is the prophet of holiness. In his book the word "holiness" as an adjective describing God is used more frequently than in all of the other Old Testament books together. For example, the term "Holy One of Israel" is used 25 times in Isaiah but only seven times in the rest of the Old Testament.

And so, the "Holiness" theme or strand is introduced in chapter six where Isaiah recounts his initial call into ministry through a heavenly vision. Isaiah explains the notion of holiness in three different ways:

A. Holiness and Transcendence

> [1] In the year of King Uzziah's death I saw the Lord sitting on a throne, lofty and exalted, with the train

> of His robe filling the temple. ² Seraphim stood above Him, each having six wings: with two he covered his face, and with two he covered his feet, and with two he flew. ³ And one called out to another and said,
> "Holy, Holy, Holy, is the Lord of hosts,
> The whole earth is full of His glory."
> - Isaiah 6:1-3

Here, Isaiah sees God as an exalted King with the ceaseless call of the angels crying out, "Holy, Holy, Holy." This is a heavenly vision which was not comparable to anything he had ever seen on earth (it was transcendent - it surpassed earthly/physical reality).

B. Holiness and Judgement

> ⁴ And the foundations of the thresholds trembled at the voice of him who called out, while the temple was filling with smoke. ⁵ Then I said,
> "Woe is me, for I am ruined!
> Because I am a man of unclean lips,
> And I live among a people of unclean lips;
> For my eyes have seen the King, the Lord of hosts."
> - Isaiah 6:4-5

Next, Isaiah realizes the deadly result for one who is unholy and who comes into contact with or into the presence of the

One who is Holy. He knows that mixing the holy with the unholy results in death.

C. Holiness and Salvation

> ⁶ Then one of the seraphim flew to me with a burning coal in his hand, which he had taken from the altar with tongs. ⁷ He touched my mouth with it and said, "Behold, this has touched your lips; and your iniquity is taken away and your sin is forgiven."
> - Isaiah 6:6-7

Finally, we see one of the seraphs taking a hot coal from the altar and purging Isaiah's uncleanness thus saving his life and enabling him to stand in the presence of the Holy God. This action demonstrates that man has no power to save or ability to make himself holy. Salvation, cleansing and holiness come from God through His appointed servant (in this case, the Seraph who is at the highest level of angelic beings and associated with light or fire) and who prefigures Christ.

The concept/strand of the "holiness" of God is found throughout Isaiah's prophecies in the various ways his visions portray God:

- The Holy One as Creator - 41:20
- The Holy One as Potter - 45:9
- The Holy One as Maker - 45:11

The main storyline in the use of the Holy One strand is the rejection by the Jewish people of this Holy One and the judgment as a result (5:24). This is followed by the Holy One as Savior who invites the people to return to God (30:15). The idea of the Holy One is woven throughout the book and combined with portraits of the Messianic hope which we saw in the previous chapter and was the first of these five strands.

- The "Messianic Hope" as King - 6:1-3
- The "Messianic Hope" as Conqueror - 60:14

> "The sons of those who afflicted you will come bowing to you,
> And all those who despised you will bow themselves at the soles of your feet;
> And they will call you the city of the Lord,
> The Zion of the Holy One of Israel.
> - Isaiah 60:14

The overarching storyline that uses these metaphors, portraits or strands to tell its story really has three parts:

- Part 1 - The awesome threat posed by a holy God exposed to a careless, unworthy, rejecting and unresponsive people - Chapters 1-37
- Part 2 - The length to which the Holy One will go to deal with sin, reclaim the sinner and create a righteous people for Himself - Chapters 40-53

- o Chapters 38-39 are historical in nature
- Part 3 - The eternal state of holiness which the Holy One will prepare for those who respond to Him which will last forever - Chapters 56-66

Let us now examine the fourth strand that Isaiah uses to tell his story.

History and Faith

This strand deals with the actual events taking place during Isaiah's ministry and highlights the history and faith of the Jewish people.

A. History

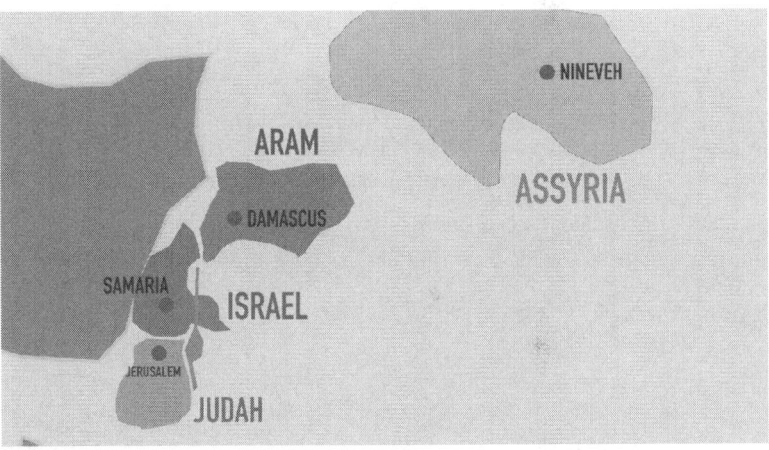

Isaiah prophesied during the reigns of four kings:

1. **Uzziah** - died - 740/739 BC - Isiah is called
2. **Jotham** - 740/739 - 732/731 BC
3. **Ahaz** - 732/731 - 716/715 BC
4. **Hezekiah** - 716/715 - 687/686 BC

The Northern Kingdom of Israel and later the Southern Kingdom of Judah were each in turn affected (threatened) by the expansionist plans of Assyria and later on those of Babylon.

Isaiah served at a time when the threats to two kings, Ahaz and Hezekiah, came from these two world powers.

1. Crisis Under Ahaz - (732-716 BC)

> ^{1} Now it came about in the days of Ahaz, the son of Jotham, the son of Uzziah, king of Judah, that Rezin the king of Aram and Pekah the son of Remaliah, king of Israel, went up to Jerusalem to wage war against it, but could not conquer it. ^{2} When it was reported to the house of David, saying, "The Arameans have camped in Ephraim," his heart and the hearts of his people shook as the trees of the forest shake with the wind.
>
> ^{3} Then the Lord said to Isaiah, "Go out now to meet Ahaz, you and your son Shear-jashub, at the end of the conduit of the upper pool, on the highway to the fuller's field, ^{4} and say to him, 'Take care and be

> calm, have no fear and do not be fainthearted because of these two stubs of smoldering firebrands, on account of the fierce anger of Rezin and Aram and the son of Remaliah. ⁵ Because Aram, with Ephraim and the son of Remaliah, has planned evil against you, saying, ⁶ "Let us go up against Judah and terrorize it, and make for ourselves a breach in its walls and set up the son of Tabeel as king in the midst of it," ⁷ thus says the Lord God: "It shall not stand nor shall it come to pass. ⁸ For the head of Aram is Damascus and the head of Damascus is Rezin (now within another 65 years Ephraim will be shattered, so that it is no longer a people), ⁹ and the head of Ephraim is Samaria and the head of Samaria is the son of Remaliah. If you will not believe, you surely shall not last.""
> - Isaiah 7:1-9

The nations to the immediate north of Judah (Israel/Ephraim and Aram) were united in order to protect themselves against their own northern threat, Assyria. These two (Israel and Aram) tried to invade and overtake Judah but failed to do so. A second invasion by the same powers was tried but this time the goal was to conquer the people and depose of the King (Ahaz) and replace him with another (non-Davidic) King (Son of Tabeel - vs. 6) thus creating a three-nation block to defend against Assyrian expansionism.

The true threat here was the notion of ending the divinely appointed lineage of Kings from David's family through military means. It is at this point that Isaiah brings a message from God to Ahaz the Jewish King on David's throne.

In short, the message is to do nothing and wait on God and decide:

- If God sees the Kingdom of Judah like other worldly Kingdoms dependent on military might for survival,
- or is Judah and its King dependent on God for its survival.

We learn that Ahaz chose to make an alliance with Assyria. In an exchange for submission to Assyria, he gave up the freedom and independence/sovereignty of his throne to gain Assyria's protection from Judah's immediate northern enemies, Israel and Aram. Ahaz does this despite Isaiah's prophecy that God would destroy both of these northern threats in the near future.

2. Crisis Under Hezekiah - (716-687 BC)

We learn that the two northern powers fell just as Isaiah had prophesied to Ahaz.

- Damascus (Aram) - 732 BC
- Samaria (Israel/Ephraim) - 722 BC

The Assyrian empire was now a major and immediate threat, and Egypt to the south wanted to form a military alliance with Judah (Southern Kingdom) in order to defend against their mutual enemy to the north, Assyria. Isaiah counseled Hezekiah, the king at that time, against forming such an alliance since Judah's defender was God, not a human power (Egypt).

Assyria, led by Sennacherib, eventually attacked Judah once it declared its independence and easily crushed the effort that Egypt made to come to Judah's defense. Hezekiah surrendered and asked for terms of peace with Assyria and in response was forced to pay a huge tribute in exchange for the cessation of war.

However, once the payment was made the Assyrians treacherously violated the condition of the surrender treaty and attacked Jerusalem anyways. Hezekiah belatedly accepted Isaiah's inspired counsel to trust in God for his safety and survival. We read that the city was saved and the Assyrians returned north and both their empire and power began to decline, and eventually were defeated by the Babylonians in 612 BC (Isaiah 37:36-38).

B. Faith

The second part/theme of this fourth strand deals with Isaiah's visions concerning two periods in Judah's history.

Chapters 40-48 – The period when God's people are saved through the actions and edicts of King Cyrus (Medo-Persian King who released the Jews from Babylonian captivity and returned them to Jerusalem from exile in Babylon).

Isaiah does not provide a history for this but he speaks of it through prophecy and visions of this event taking place. It is an eschatological vision of their ultimate freedom from physical bondage.

In chapters 49 to 55, Isaiah describes the visions representing the people's spiritual freedom from their captivity of sin. It is here that he introduces the Suffering Servant who is the One who will accomplish this liberation through the sacrifice of Himself. He is the Messianic Hope not as King, not as Conqueror, but this time, the Messianic Hope as Servant.

The full gospel message of the completeness of sin, weakness and inability to save self, manner of salvation (vicarious atonement), the identity of the Savior, etc. are all contained in Isaiah's prophecy concerning the Suffering Servant. It also includes the necessity of waiting for this event patiently and expectantly until it's sure arrival.

A third and final section (chapters 56 to 66) continues Isaiah's description of the Lord's people, aware of their need, waiting for the Anointed One who will fulfill God's requirements for salvation on their behalf. The prophet ends his book with a picture of people praying, waiting and hoping for the eternal glory of a new creation.

Isaiah emphasizes the central theme of this fourth as well as every other of the five strands of thought that makes up his book - faith, a faith that persists, prays and waits in hope.

> [22] "For just as the new heavens and the new earth
> Which I make will endure before Me," declares the Lord,
> "So your offspring and your name will endure.
> [23] "And it shall be from new moon to new moon
> And from sabbath to sabbath,
> All mankind will come to bow down before Me," says the Lord.
> - Isaiah 66:22-23

In our next chapter, we will cover the fifth and final strand - literary structures and features. A better understanding of the literary devices that Isaiah uses will help the reader accurately discern the Prophet's message.

4. Structures and Features
Part 3

We've noted that the Book of Isaiah is not a history or narrative like the Book of Acts where Luke provides a historical narrative of the establishment of the church in Jerusalem at the early part of the 1st century and goes forward to describe key events and characters in its development up to Paul's imprisonment in Rome in about 64 AD. Luke's narrative spans a period from about 33 AD to 64 AD, all of which is linear, concise, historical, easy to plot on a graph, follow and understand.

Isaiah is completely different. Aside from a few chapters of historical information at the midpoint of the book, Isaiah's writings are the product of visions and prophecies recorded in poetic form. He writes about the impending judgment of God on His unfaithful people in the form of invasion by foreign powers, and the salvation and blessings that will eventually come through a future Messiah, who he describes in detail.

These prophetic utterances are contained in five different themes or strands which are braided together to form a single image in the end and that image is Jesus Christ.

And so, in this chapter we will examine the fifth of these five strands:

1. The Messianic hope as:
    1. King
    2. Servant
    3. Anointed Conqueror
2. The City (Jerusalem)
    1. Metaphor for God's people (present, future, end-times)
3. The Holy One of Israel
    1. A Holy God is: Transcendent, Judge, Savior
    2. A Holy God as: Creator, Potter, Maker
4. The History and Faith of the Jewish People
    1. Ahaz - Faithless
    2. Hezekiah - Faithful
5. The Literary and Structural Features of Isaiah

Literary and Structural Features of Isaiah

This strand is not about the actual content of the Book of Isaiah but rather how that content was put together. To understand the writings properly requires understanding of how Isaiah arranged the material in his book and the various devices that he used in his writings.

The following is not a complete list but some of the important literary features to consider:

1. Mosaic vs. Linear

As I mentioned before, if you read the Gospels or the Book of Acts, you are reading a linear narrative. They begin with Jesus' birth or ministry (Gospels) or the establishment of the church (Acts) and tell the story to the end (Gospels - Jesus' resurrection/ascension/ Acts - Establishment of the church throughout the Roman Empire).

If you read Isaiah with this mindset, you will quickly become confused and bored because his book is set up as a mosaic and not a linear narrative.

A mosaic is a whole piece made with disparate parts. Linear books follow a historical and chronological order. Mosaics, on the other hand, use events, poetry, prophecy, history and prayers (to name a few, but not all of the elements) in order to create a single image or portrait, or tell a story, or in the case of Isaiah, convey a message from God to His chosen people.

2. Literary Features

We know that Hebrew poetry and literature used various features to give their writing texture, emotion and aids in understanding the exact meeting in context.

A. Parallelism

A good example of this was the use of a device called parallelism used extensively in the Psalms, as well as other Old Testament books including Isaiah. For example, the author of a Psalm would repeat the same thought or idea using different words in successive lines of the poem. There were different types of parallelism.

Synonymous Parallelism

The second line repeats the first using different words that have the same meaning.

> [1] The heavens are telling of the glory of God;
> And their expanse is declaring the work of His hands.
> [2] Day to day pours forth speech,
> And night to night reveals knowledge.
> - Psalm 19:1-2

Synthetic Parallelism

The second line adds to the first.

> ³ Who may ascend into the hill of the Lord?
> And who may stand in His holy place?
> ⁴ He who has clean hands and a pure heart,
> Who has not lifted up his soul to falsehood
> And has not sworn deceitfully.
> - Psalm 24:3-4

Synonymous:

- Who shall ascend the hill of the Lord
  And who shall stand in His holy place?

Synthetic:

- He who has clean hands and a pure heart
  Who does not lift up his soul to what is false
  and does not swear deceitfully.

Antithetic Parallelism

The second line contrasts the first.

> My flesh and my heart may fail,
> But God is the strength of my heart and my portion forever.
> - Isaiah 73:26

Climactic Parallelism

Successive lines build to a climax or a summary.

> **Building:**
> [17] Though the fig tree should not blossom
> And there be no fruit on the vines,
> Though the yield of the olive should fail
> And the fields produce no food,
> Though the flock should be cut off from the fold
> And there be no cattle in the stalls,
>
> **Climax/Summary:**
> [18] Yet I will exult in the Lord,
> I will rejoice in the God of my salvation.
> - Habakkuk 3:17-18

Eclectic Parallelism

A combination of different types.

> **Synonymous:**
> **Synthetic:**
> How long, O Lord, will I call for help,
> And You will not hear?
>
> **Synthetic:**
> I cry out to You, "Violence!"
> Yet You do not save.
> - Habakkuk 1:2

Emphatic Parallelism

> You shall love the Lord your God with all your <u>heart</u> and with all your <u>soul</u> and with all your <u>might</u>.
> - Deuteronomy 6:5

Three separate words referring to the same object - the whole person. To love with one is to love with all. I explain all of this to show that Isaiah also uses these as well as other devices throughout his book. For example:

B. Imagery

The imagery that Isaiah uses becomes evident when comparing different passages.

> [10] Hear the word of the Lord,
> You rulers of Sodom;
> Give ear to the instruction of our God,
> You people of Gomorrah.
> [11] "What are your multiplied sacrifices to Me?"
> Says the Lord.
> "I have had enough of burnt offerings of rams
> And the fat of fed cattle;
> And I take no pleasure in the blood of bulls, lambs or goats.
> - Isaiah 1:10-11

In this passage, even though he uses a literary device like synonymous parallelism, there is no imagery it reads like a conversation.

> "Yet you have not called on Me, O Jacob;
> But you have become weary of Me, O Israel.
> - Isaiah 43:22

Same problem with Judah but uses both devices of personification (the nation is tired of God); and also uses synonymous parallelism (second line repeats the first line but with different words - Not called / Become weary).

These devices are not loud or showy but rather low-key and easy to miss but their variety and repetition give the writing a certain texture and enables Isaiah to highlight certain ideas in a work that is complex and lengthy. Too dramatic and ornate would become wearying after several chapters, but no changes, highlights or texturing devices would lead to boredom in a work that is this long and repeats the same ideas several times.

Another literary feature in Isaiah's writing is:

The Extended Doublet

This feature is noted when Isaiah covers the same area of truth in the same consecutive steps, twice over. In other words, he tells the story, the prophecy, or the warning twice or more times using a similar order of events/lessons but he repeats it from a different perspective. Like the report of a car accident from the view of the driver of the car and then the view of a bystander.

An example of this "extended doublet" is in chapter 7. This concerns the prophecy concerning the attack on Judah and Jerusalem by the combined forces of the Northern Kingdom of Israel who joined with the Aramaeans to overtake the Southern Kingdom and its principal city of Jerusalem.

Isaiah's prophecy lists the pending attack; the need to trust the Lord; the failure of this invasion; the subsequent destruction of the Northern Kingdom by the Assyrians (722 BC), the future destruction of the Southern Kingdom by the Babylonians in 582 BC; and the eventual coming of a Savior who would be rooted in the remnant of that Southern Kingdom after its destruction and restoration. This entire order of events is addressed to the Southern Kingdom by Isaiah's prophecy in 7:1-9:7.

Now, in Isaiah 9:8-11:16, Isaiah refers to all of the same elements but this time from the point of view of the Northern Kingdom and its ultimate conqueror, Assyria. In 7:1-9:7, he speaks and records a prophecy of what is to come. In 9:8-11:16, he pronounces a judgment that will come for what the Northern Kingdom and the Aramaeans tried to do to Jerusalem - again, all to take place in the future.

In both instances, Isaiah ends his prophecies with a description of the promised Savior to come. The same promise but a different description.

In other sections of his book, Isaiah uses this repetition device, the extended doublet, for not just two but three times in reference to a single event, person or theme. For example, let's go back to our analogy of the accident. You have the driver's report of what happened, then you have the bystander's report and finally, you have the police report. Three different records of one single event. This is what Isaiah does.

- In 28:1-29:24 - the North and South Kingdoms are warned twice.

- In 30:1-35:10 - Judah is warned against making alliances with other nations and warned three times.

I mention these because understanding the types of literary devices used by the author and how they work (i.e. parallelism) helps us to discern the correct and intended meaning of the text. So we've looked at the "mosaic" layout for Isaiah's book and several of the literary features like parallelism, imagery and the extended doublet. One last point about Isaiah's writing which is often debated is:

3. Single Author vs. School of Authors

As I mentioned before, one of the main debates concerning this book is if it was written by a single person (a man called Isaiah who lived in the 8th-7th century and served as a prophet); or this is a work completed by a "school" of prophets/writers who produced the material based on Isaiah's initial work but done over a period of four centuries ending in 435 BC.

The "school of writers" theory argues that the variety of styles and devices in Isaiah's book can be explained by the fact that the book was actually written by multiple authors over a period of several centuries.

Of course, those who hold this position also use this idea as a basis to deny the possibility of predictive prophecy. For these people, the "school of prophets/writers" producing material over a number of centuries theory provides a rational answer to explain the many prophetical sections in Isaiah. They see Isaiah's book as history and not prophecy.

On the other hand, the "single author" understanding of Isaiah requires no special explanation since Isaiah is a known historical figure who lived and had access to the people and the events that he writes about, not to mention that the book itself is presented as the work of a single author.

Of course, for those who believe that God used prophets, like Isaiah, Daniel, Jeremiah and others to communicate to the

Jews and through them to communicate to us who believe today, the single author idea presents no challenge of faith.

For those who believe the idea that a man spoke accurately from God about the present, near future, distant future and the end times, is an acceptable and natural demonstration of the work of the Holy Spirit in one of God's servants - in this case, a man named Isaiah.

To properly understand the content and appreciate the power of Isaiah's book, we must see that it is a mosaic fashioned from parts of poetry, history, prophecy and narrative all combined to fashion a single message from God relevant to every generation of His people starting with the Jews in the days of King Uzziah to the members of the Lord's church today.

Summary and Outline

Isaiah uses a variety of literary devices and historical narrative that are used as a framework for his messages and prophecies from God to the Jewish people and surrounding nations.

As I mentioned in a previous chapter, Isaiah's book can be divided into three main sections:

1. Messages relating to God's judgment - Chapters 1-35
2. The historical account of Hezekiah's reign - Chapters 36-39
3. Messages relating to God's mercy - Chapters 40-66

If, as you read the book, you feel that it is gloomy and harsh, this is because more than half of it deals with warnings and judgments against the Northern and Southern Kingdoms, as well as a dozen or so surrounding nations.

Of course, it's not all doom and gloom. Mixed in with the judgments are the promises of a savior, the story of God rescuing Hezekiah and Jerusalem from a sure destruction by a foreign army, and a comprehensive description of the Messiah. In addition to these Isaiah also explains in detail the way that the Messiah would achieve salvation and the nature of that salvation. Isaiah provides more precise information concerning man's ultimate salvation in his book than anywhere else in the Old Testament.

Detailed Outline of Isaiah (TruthSaves.org)

Introduction: 1:1

I. Messages Relating to Judgment 1-35

1. The opening call of God 1
    1. To Judah 1:2-20
    2. To Jerusalem 1:21-31
2. A word concerning Judah and Jerusalem 2-5
3. The Introduction to the Coming Messiah 6-12
    1. The Vision of the LORD and the Holy Seed 6
    2. The Great Sign — a Virgin 7
    3. Immanuel, a Stone of Stumbling to Israel and Judah 8
    4. The Light from Galilee, a Child 9:1-7
    5. The Light, a Destroyer of the enemies 9:8-10:34
    6. The Rod and Branch, the Root, and the Future Day 11
    7. The Holy One 12
4. The Burdens Against the Nations 13-23
    1. Against Babylon 13-14:27
    2. Against Philistia 14:28-32
    3. Against Moab 15-16
    4. Against Damascus 17
    5. Against Ethopia 18
    6. Against Egypt 19-20
    7. Against the Wilderness of the Sea 21:1-10
    8. Against Dumah (Edom) 21:11-12
    9. Against Arabia 21:13-17

            10. Against the Valley of Vision 22
            11. Agaisnt Tyre 23
     5. The Woes and deliverance 24-35
            1. The earth will be destroyed 24
            2. But there is victory over death 25
            3. For those who trust in the LORD 26
            4. He delivers 27
            5. Woe to the drunkards of Ephraim 28:1-15
            6. There will be a precious cornerstone 28:16-29
            7. Woe to Jerusalem 29-30:11
            8. God is gracious 30:12-33
            9. Woe to those who rely upon Egypt 31
            10. There will be a king of righteousness 32
            11. Woe to evil-doers 33:1-16
            12. There is coming a beautiful king 34:17 to 35

II. Historical Account of Hezekiah 36-39
     1. Sennacherib's boast 36
     2. God's Intervention 37
     3. Hezekiah's Illness 38
     4. Hezekiah's Sin 39

III. Messages Relating to Mercy 40-66
     1. The Revelation of God 40-48
     2. The Revelation of the Servant 49-53
     3. The Call for Righteous Living 54-59
     4. The Reign of Messiah 60-66

https://truthsaves.org/bible-book-outlines/outline-of-isaiah/

This outline is a guide in reading the book since with it you always know the context of what Isaiah is talking about. The key idea in Isaiah is that the Messiah is coming even though the term "Messiah" is only used in reference to "Cyrus" King of the Medes/Persians (Isaiah 45:1).

We will not do a line-by-line study from here forward but will select key passages to present a variety of lessons using Isaiah as our springboard. You now have a detailed outline and information on the features to guide you as you read the book of Isaiah.

5.
When Good Becomes Evil and Evil Becomes Good

Isaiah 5:20

> Woe to those who call evil good, and good evil;
> Who substitute darkness for light and light for darkness;
> Who substitute bitter for sweet and sweet for bitter!
> - Isaiah 5:20

In this particular verse the prophet Isaiah is describing one of the sins that the Jewish people are guilty of that will ultimately lead to the destruction of the Northern Kingdom by the

Assyrians in 720 BC, and later on to the destruction of the Southern Kingdom by the Babylonians in 586 BC.

This was not the only sin mentioned in this passage; abuse of alcohol, immoral revelry, dishonesty, corruption and arrogance before God were other violations that were cited. These things were serious enough but in verse 20 Isaiah describes not just a sinful act but rather what this sinful nation had come to: they were so wicked and proud that they celebrated and promoted what was essentially evil and labeled as evil what had traditionally been seen as good.

Isaiah was telling the people that they had completely reversed the moral order and that God would punish them for this. It wasn't simply that they had failed to obey or comply to God's moral order, nothing new there, people had always failed in this regard. What was new was their attempt to actually change the order itself so that sinfulness was now considered acceptable, and holiness, faith and obedience were to be rejected.

Isaiah was warning them that once they headed down this road the only result would be destruction. Destruction because if they completely rejected God's moral order and created one of their own, they would no longer be of any use to Him as His chosen people.

Trying but failing to obey God's commands left them depending on God's mercy and strength for life and salvation, and this was acceptable to God. Making up and following their own laws and moral framework would, as history shows, lead to a complete shattering of their nation.

The Supreme Court's Decision

We don't use the term "call evil good and good evil" anymore. Today we have more subtle ways of deconstructing the moral order set by God in His Word. We say things like:

- love is what matters
- every lifestyle deserves respect
- we must guarantee everyone's rights
- gender equality
- marriage equality
- a woman's right to choose
- and my personal favorite: "You don't want to be on the wrong side of history do you?" Meaning you need to keep up with the "new" order, or else pay the consequences.

Don't get me wrong, these terms are legitimate in themselves. Love does matter and we must respect everyone and this idea is often guaranteed by Law. But these terms have been hijacked by godless ideologues who use them to recreate the moral order of our nation into something that would have been unrecognizable to most Americans 75 years ago, and contrary to God's Word in any generation. I don't need to drag out a laundry list of social ills that plague our nation to make my point, one example can serve to represent the rest.

On June 26, 2015, the Supreme Court in a 5-4 decision, made marriage between two men or two women legal in all 50 states.

I don't have the time to list all the twisted arguments, political pressures and likely fall-out from this ruling in this short book. Suffice to say that American society, groomed by decades of morally decadent entertainment, misinformed by a secular news media and educational system, and brainwashed by a wealthy and politically well-connected Gay lobby actually bought into the **ridiculous** premise that two men or two women should be able to marry each other with all the rights and privileges that heterosexual couples have.

I say ridiculous because the one basis that all cultures and religions throughout history have agreed on is that marriage is the best environment or relationship to have and raise children.

I say ridiculous because this is the only thing Gay couples cannot do! They can marry, have sex, build a house, live together for 100 years, yes they can even love each other; but they cannot naturally produce a child which is the essential, human, moral and social reason for marriage in the first place!

I could say immoral, unbiblical, unchristian and defend each argument, but I say ridiculous because Gay marriage should never have passed this very lowest bar of credibility.

However, five lawyers who embodied the entire social and intellectual waste of this generation's foolish thinking decided to change the moral order set by God and followed by all societies for thousands of years. Isaiah spoke of these when he said:

> Woe to those who are wise in their own eyes
> And clever in their own sight!
> - Isaiah 5:21

These three women and two men on the Supreme Court who voted in this way have now enshrined in law a new standard for what is right and what is wrong when it comes to not only marriage, but sexual expression as well.

I'm not one to predict the end of this nation or the time it would take place, God decides these things, but when I saw a picture of the White House lit up in the rainbow colors of the Gay pride movement on the front page of the USA Today newspaper, I knew that something profound had taken place in our country, and there would be no going back to where we once were.

The Wrong Side of History

The proponents of same-sex marriage from the President to the Judges and most news and entertainment personalities love to warn Christians that we're on the wrong side of history in this matter.

They compare this ruling to the emancipation of the slaves after the Civil War, or the right to vote for women. Their argument is that those who are against same-sex marriage today are like the ones who were for slavery in the past or those who didn't want women to have the right to vote. Talk about the wrong side of history!

This accusation coming from people who have ignored and perverted history in order to force their fake civil rights agenda down the throat of an uninformed and gullible nation. The diabolic cleverness of their argument is that they are correct in stating the fact that not allowing Gay couples to marry is discrimination.

For example, not allowing marriage between black and white people, this is discrimination. Not allowing a woman to vote because she is a woman is discrimination. Paying a handicapped accountant less then a non-handicapped accountant is discrimination.

So in this sense they have a correct **way** to argue their case. For example, if a man and woman can marry, it is discrimination not to let two men or two women marry. After all, they are consenting adults who love each other.

Please do not misunderstand, I said that they have found a correct way to argue their case; an argument based on the principle of civil and human rights. But the argument itself is false: civil or human rights protection is given to those who are by nature or some event brought into a certain condition or status.

In other words, a situation or status over which you have no choice (i.e. you are born or become handicapped in some way, your gender or culture). These are things you have no control over and there are legal protections set in place so that you are not abused or discriminated against just because you are a woman, you are black or you are handicapped in some way.

For many years homosexuals tried to gain acceptance for their lifestyle by using the scientific argument that they were just born that way; it was genetics. They touted research (much of it done by gay researchers) that "suggested" that there might be a link between homosexual behavior and biology. The problem was that they never found the genetic "silver bullet" that proved the existence of a "Gay gene" and if you had it, you would automatically be disposed to homosexuality.

The strongest argument against the "Gay gene" theory was the result of the famous twins research. Here I will read from the report on this research:

> "Eight major studies of more than 10,000 sets of identical twins during the last two decades all arrive at the same conclusion: Gays were not born that way. 'At best, genetics is a minor factor,' says Dr. Neil Whitehead, PhD in biochemistry and statistics. Identical twins have the same genes or DNA and they are nurtured in equal prenatal conditions. Therefore, if homosexuality is caused by genetics or prenatal conditions and one twin is gay, the co-twin should also be gay. If both twins are not gay, then homosexuality cannot be genetically dictated. "The predominant things that create homosexuality in one identical twin and not in the other <u>have to be post-birth factors.</u>" Same-sex attraction (homosexuality) is caused by non-shared factors — things that happen to one twin but not the other, or a personal response to an event by one of the twins and not the other."
> - *My Genes Made Me Do It!:*
> *Homosexuality and the Scientific Evidence*
> *Neil Whitehead and Briar Whitehead*

This is just one of many scientific studies that concluded that genetics had little or no effect on same-sex attraction. The consensus continues to be that same-sex attraction develops when a person is exposed to various experiences and situations as they grow up; for example, homes with no father or a dominant mother and weak father, early exposure to pornography (especially Gay pornography), sexual and physical abuse, same-sex experimentation during puberty, sexual confusion or anxiety, or a permissive society that encourages this lifestyle.

Not everyone who experiences these things becomes Gay, but many of these factors are present in the lives of those who experience same-sex attraction.

Seeing that the scientific argument was going nowhere, the Gay movement switched tactics and began a push to find legitimacy using human and civil rights arguments. They cast themselves as victims of discrimination, tied their wagon to the American Civil Rights Movement, and pressured government using this new approach.

This is why I say that the way they argue is effective (it convinced the media, courts, President and public opinion), but the substance of their argument is false and here's why: to achieve the status of a discriminated against minority, one has to show that their condition is due to:

1. Genetics – race, gender, handicap, etc.
2. Events – accident/injury, loss of ability, etc.
3. Condition – black and poor, ex-convict, immigrant, etc.

Homosexuals fail to qualify in any of these categories.

1. Homosexuality is not the result of genetics. This is not just my opinion, this is scientific fact!
2. No one forces one to become gay, it is a condition that evolves slowly, mostly based on experience, environment and decisions made.
3. Gays are not a downtrodden minority needing protection. They do and have wielded more influence than any other group that at most comprises of about 2% of the total population (Whitehead's research also shows that about 50% of the gay population drifts back to heterosexual behavior as they grow older).

So the point I am making is that Gays have won a significant legal victory by successfully using a false argument to make same-sex marriage possible in all 50 states.

When they say, "You don't want to be on the wrong side of history, do you?" this is just the shorthand way of tying their cause with the civil rights movement and casting those who disagree as racists, prejudiced and narrow-minded relics of the past. Don't be fooled by their slippery rhetoric and false argument.

Where to Now?

The big question among Christians now that the ruling of the court has come down is, "Where to now?" How do we change this ruling? What kind of laws should we create to protect churches, ministers and Christian institutions like schools and colleges against lawsuits and other attacks?

I suppose these things need to be considered, but for most of us Christians who are not lawyers or responsible for Christian-based organizations, what do we do in the face of this change in the moral order of our country? Here are some suggestions:

1. Stop being surprised and discouraged at what an unbelieving and unregenerated world does!

> ¹ Therefore, since Christ has suffered in the flesh, arm yourselves also with the same purpose, because he who has suffered in the flesh has ceased from sin, ² so as to live the rest of the time in the flesh no longer for the lusts of men, but for the will of God. ³ For the time already past is sufficient for you to have carried out the desire of the Gentiles, having pursued a course of sensuality, lusts, drunkenness, carousing, drinking parties and abominable idolatries. ⁴ In all this, they are surprised that you do not run with them into the same excesses of dissipation, and they malign you; ⁵ but they will give account to Him who is ready to judge the living and the dead.
> - I Peter 4:1-5

From the very beginning, the church has been at odds with the world; Peter is reminding his readers of the status quo that existed then and continues until now. What did you think would happen when the Supreme Court refused to hear or give credit to any argument for traditional marriage based on the Bible? You could argue your case from any point of view except from the Bible's point of view. What kind of law did you think would be created when the judges refused to take into consideration any direction supplied by the original Law-Giver?

In this world there is only discouragement and turmoil, don't let that reality get you down. Remember what Jesus said in John 16:33b: "In the world you have tribulation, but take courage; I have overcome the world."

2. Stop worrying about the decline of the world – it's normal!

Christians stress over the decline of morality, values and conduct in their world. They worry if their grandchildren will be able to survive. The moral condition of the world goes up and down in a cyclical fashion. There were times that were terrible (Roman Empire, Middle Ages) and times that were, relatively speaking, good (after WWII in America). But the pendulum swings between the two extremes and will continue to do so until Jesus comes.

> [36] "But of that day and hour no one knows, not even the angels of heaven, nor the Son, but the Father

> alone. [37] For the coming of the Son of Man will be just like the days of Noah. [38] For as in those days before the flood they were eating and drinking, marrying and giving in marriage, until the day that Noah entered the ark, [39] and they did not understand until the flood came and took them all away; so will the coming of the Son of Man be.
> - Matthew 24:36-39

The thing to be concerned about is not the condition of an unbelieving and wicked world; no, the thing to focus on is our own readiness. Unlike the world, we know that Jesus is coming and we know how to be ready for Him. The Bible has already told us that the world won't be ready, it will come by surprise; no need to stress out over that. Just make sure you are ready!

3. Stop trying to "fix" the world.

There are any number of organizations who are trying to fix things: the environment, the poor, immigrants, rights of women, Gays, Black Lives Matter, etc. I'm not saying that these and other efforts are wasted or not worthy, Christianity needs to affect the world in a positive and constructive way like salt and light. But these things don't achieve our primary goal as a church which is the salvation of souls. Jesus didn't tell us to go out and "fix" the world, He told us to call all people to come out of the world and into the kingdom of God, which is the church.

We can't save the world, it is already set for destruction when Jesus comes. We can only provide the means to escape the world and the sure destruction it will suffer, and that is through the gospel of Jesus Christ. There is no fixing the world, there is only coming out of it.

Summary

In closing I'd like to acknowledge that we **are** on the wrong side of history, the history being written by this unbelieving generation:

- Just like Noah was on the wrong side of history for 100 years...till it started to rain.
- Just like Isaiah who largely spoke of things few of any of his generation understood.
- Just like Jeremiah who was ignored for most of his life and ministry...till the invading armies showed up.
- Just like Jesus was seemingly silenced for three days and three nights...till resurrection Sunday.

I'd rather be on the wrong side of history written by man than the wrong side of God and what is written in His book of life!

So let's not be discouraged or afraid. This may be a time of testing and pruning for the church, for ourselves and our faith. Is losing our tax-exempt status going to keep us from going to church? Let us not compromise what we know to be true about marriage from God's Word.

We need to find ways to articulate this without being mean-spirited or angry. Much of what turns people against us is not simply our Bible teachings, it's our self-righteous and mean-spirited attitude at times. It is unfortunate that there are times when homosexuals cannot see Christ in us and so it makes it easy for them to reject Him because of us.

Never mind the world and its wickedness, let us simply focus on what we're supposed to be doing.

Let us be about our Father's business. Not fixing the world or being discouraged by the sin in the world, but rather preaching the Good News to the world. If we are busy doing this, we won't be burdened by the other.

Isaiah has gone before us warning that there would be times when evil would be considered good and good evil. We are living in those times. However, as Christians, we know what to do. Let's get busy doing it.

6.
Here Am I, Send Me Answering the Call to Ministry

Isaiah 6:8-9

One of the most difficult decisions I ever had to make was the decision to leave my job as a Customer Service Manager for a large pharmaceutical company and go into full-time ministry (40+ years ago). There were so many questions that had no clear-cut answers; so many doubts about my ability; so much anxiety over how things would work out. When I finally arrived at Oklahoma Christian University for training, I found that most other people going into ministry felt pretty much the same way. And, it wasn't only those going into preaching but other men and women considering going into the mission field as well as brothers thinking about becoming deacons or serving as elders.

Somehow when the call to ministry comes (whatever it may be in the church), there comes with it a lot of difficult questions. For this reason, I'd like to review Isaiah the prophet's call into ministry. Hopefully, we can find direction and encouragement for the men and women that are being called into the various ministries that the church needs in every generation.

Background of Isaiah

The Prophet

Most of what we know about Isaiah himself comes from chapters 6-8; 36-39 of his book. He was the son of Amoz (not to be confused with Amos the prophet). There is, however, no information on Amoz. Isaiah lived and ministered in Jerusalem for 53 years from before 739 BC (the year King Uzziah died) to after 686 BC (the year King Hezekiah died). Isaiah wrote biographies of both kings which are referenced in II Chronicles (II Chronicles 26:22; 32:32). He was married and had at least two children who had symbolic names used in his prophetic work.

- **Shear - Jashub** = "A remanent shall return" - A name given to convey hope that Judah would survive an attack by its enemies and one day return to rebuild their city.

- **Maher-Shalal-Hash-Baz** = The spoil speeds/the prey hastens"

This name referred to the coming destiny upon Judah's enemies, Syria and the Northern Kingdom of Israel.

Based on the familiarity Isaiah had with the inner workings of the temple and his proximity to the royal court, it is believed that he may have been a priest. He was well educated as can be seen in his writing style. His position and education suggests that he was wealthy and part of the upper class of Judean society of that time.

Isaiah was one of the few prophets who had disciples (Isaiah 8:16). His relationship with them may have been similar to that which Samuel and Elisha had with the "sons of the prophets" or that Jeremiah had with Baruch. They may have assisted in his ministry or helped perpetuate it as scribes.

We don't know for certain where or how he died but as non-inspired work called "The Ascension of Isaiah," says that he was executed by King Manasseh by being sawn in two. He may be the one referred to by the Hebrew writer in Hebrews 11:37 who describes heroes of the faith: "They were stoned, they were sawn in two, others were killed with the sword." That particular reference may be to the way Isaiah died.

The Times

Of course, to understand any prophet requires a view of the times that he lived in and the conditions under which he operated. There were three elements that influenced the substance of Isaiah's ministry and preaching:

1. Prosperity - King Uzziah's reign (780-740 BC) was one of great prosperity. In the midst of this wealth, Isaiah denounced the manner that this wealth was acquired, usually by the oppression of the poor. In addition to this, the wealthy were more easily exposed to and influenced by the idolatrous practices of their neighbors.

2. Strategic Location of Judah - Judah was situated geographically midway between the two superpowers of the day who constantly wanted to overrun its territory in order to stage wars against each other and neighboring countries. Isaiah continually warned the Judean kings not to form partnerships with either one of these, but rather to trust in God for their safety. Much of his prophesies had to do with warnings against such alliances and the eventual judgment of these and other nations by God.

3. Conduct of the Kings - Isaiah's training and position made him a natural choice to be God's prophet or "minister" to the kings. Much of his work was dictated by the faith and conduct of the kings he ministered to:

- **Uzziah** was at the end of his reign and died the year Isaiah was called. Uzziah was an able ruler and the Kingdom enjoyed prosperity under him. He mostly obeyed the Lord until later in his reign he sinned by improperly entering into the temple to burn incense and was struck with leprosy for his sin. Isaiah spoke out during this time condemning the oppression of the poor by the rich. (Isaiah 1:23)

- **Jotham**, Uzziah's son, succeeded him. He was also a good man who feared God, but during his reign, the idolatry that existed during his father's time was tolerated and grew worse in his day. Isaiah condemned these practices and warned of the punishment to come because of their unfaithfulness. (Isaiah 1:29-31)

- **Ahaz** succeeded Jotham and was an evil king who, against Isaiah's counsel, made alliances with foreign powers in order to defend the kingdom. Much of Isaiah's work during this period involved him warning the king against such things but also prophesying about the destruction of the Northern Kingdom and foreign nations as well. Despite these dire warnings, Isaiah continued to mix into his prophecies the future hope of a Messiah and the eventual restoration of the southern kingdom.

- The last king to receive ministry from Isaiah was **Hezekiah**. He was a reformer and tried to right many of the evils of his father, Ahaz. However, he continued the practice of forming alliances with regional powers for military reasons. It is during this period that Isaiah speaks of Judah's exile in Babylon, its eventual restoration and some of the most explicit prophecies concerning the Messiah's coming contained in the Old Testament. His final prophecies, referring to a time beyond Hezekiah's life speak of Babylon's downfall and the final triumph of God's will and purpose in the world. Isaiah was a man fully engaged in the events of his time as a servant of God called to a special ministry.

So now that we've had a brief overview of his life and times, let's focus on the subject of our lesson, his call to ministry and in what way his calling might resemble our own at this time in history.

Isaiah's Call to Ministry
– Isaiah 6:1-11

> Vs. 1a — In the year of King Uzziah's death

It is interesting to note that Isaiah mentions King Uzziah's death because it not only fixes the historic date of his vision (739 BC) but also his state of mind. Uzziah prospered as long as he followed the Lord but he eventually disobeyed God and had a tragic finish, dying as a leper in isolation. Isaiah had reason to be discouraged and disillusioned in all of this and thus was called at a time of national crisis. The king was dead, a new unproven ruler was on the throne, enemies were growing stronger and the nation was drifting into idolatry. Where was God in all of this?

Isaiah's Vision

> Vs. 1b-4 — I saw the Lord sitting on a throne, lofty and exalted, with the train of His robe filling the temple. ² Seraphim stood above Him, each having six wings: with two he covered his face, and with two he covered his feet, and with two he flew. ³ And one called out to another and said, "Holy, Holy, Holy, is the Lord of hosts, The whole earth is full of His glory." ⁴ And the foundations of the thresholds trembled at the voice of him who called out, while the temple was filling with smoke.

The answer to Isaiah's question, of course, was that God was on His throne and was allowing Isaiah a glimpse or a vision of the heavenly realm. Earthly rulers, weak with sins might die or be deposed but God was always on His throne. Almost everyone in the Bible who had a vision of heaven saw a throne. For example:

- Michaiah saw God's throne – I Kings 22:19

- Job saw God's throne – Job 26:9
- David saw God's throne – Psalms 9:4
- Daniel saw it – Daniel 7:9
- John the Apostle mentions it more than 35 times in the book of Revelation

Isaiah may have been discouraged because a great leader was no longer on the throne, but God shows Isaiah that there is no reason to worry because He is on His throne. Some other features of the vision show the power and sovereignty of God's position:

1. The train of His robe filled the temple. Kings wore robes with long trains to demonstrate their power and position. For example:

- They needed attendants to carry and arrange their robe and train when they moved around — this demonstrated how important this person was.
- This is where the idea of a long train on a wedding dress comes from — the bride is portrayed as a "queen" for that day.
- In Isaiah's vision God's train is so long that it fills the entire temple — the most sacred of all places!

2. Angels (Seraphim) were attending Him. Kings have ministers or military commanders attending them, people of

high stature. God has angels (beings even more powerful than any human being) attending Him. The term "Seraphim" means burning ones. Ezekiel describes them in this way:

> Their appearance was like burning coals of fire, like the appearance of torches going back and forth among the creatures. The fire was bright, and out of the fire went lightening.
> - Ezekiel 1:13

In addition to this, Isaiah adds that they had 6 wings. John the Apostle also says the same about six wings in Revelation 8.

- Two wings cover their face (an act of humility demonstrating that they, like us, are too low to look upon the face of God).

- Two wings to cover their feet, another gesture of humility signifying that even though they are powerful beings, they are still "created" beings and hide their most humble area.

- Two wings to fly which expresses their willingness and ability to serve God.

3. The angels proclaim God's holiness. Note that the angels are not addressing the Lord directly, but are proclaiming His glory to one another.

- They say "holy" three times because there are three Persons in One God and their praise accurately reveals the nature of God.
- The angels could see God's holy influence and power extending throughout the world, even if Isaiah in his discouragement could not.

4. The temple was shaken and filled with smoke.

- Isaiah could feel (the trembling) and see the power (smoke) of God's presence among the angels.
- This was no dream! This was 3D vision!
- As a Jew, Isaiah knew that God's presence had before been manifested by a Pillar of Cloud (Exodus 13:21-22) or smoke (Exodus 19:18) at Mt. Sinai; or the cloud of God's glory that filled the temple (I Kings 8:10-12).

At a moment of possible doubt or discouragement, God reveals Himself to Isaiah in His heavenly glory to confirm that He is and remains the sovereign King of Heaven — no matter what is happening here on earth.

Isaiah's Reaction

> ⁵ Then I said,
> "Woe is me, for I am ruined!
> Because I am a man of unclean lips,

> And I live among a people of unclean lips;
> For my eyes have seen the King, the Lord of hosts."

Despite his intelligence, privilege and personal integrity and spirituality, Isaiah sees himself for what he really is, a sinful man among a sinful people. Compared to other men, he may have seemed righteous by earthly standards, but compared to the angels he was weak and small, not even able to praise God the way they did. And before God's brilliance, his own sins and failings were extremely evident and damning. He was before God without a mediator, without any covering or sacrifice and so he rightly understood that he was doomed. Think about it:

If the priests could only go into the holy of holies once per year and only after having sacrificed for themselves and the people so they would not be killed, there was no chance for him entering into the very presence of God without any preparation. Isaiah's vision of God served to bring into sharper focus his own sinful nature and sense of lostness for himself and his people.

God's Response

> ⁶ Then one of the seraphim flew to me with a burning coal in his hand, which he had taken from the altar with tongs. ⁷ He touched my mouth with it and said, "Behold, this has touched your lips; and your iniquity is taken away and your sin is forgiven."

The altar was the place where man's sins were dealt with in the temple.

- Animal sacrifices were made and burned as a "type" or preview of Christ's sacrifice to come for the sins of all men.

- The altar Isaiah sees in the heavenly place is where Christ's sacrifice continually exists before God cleansing the sins of all.

- The angel takes a burning coal (the power of purification) and touches his lips (the source of his sins and the instrument of his ministry.

- Isaiah is told the meaning and result of this action by the angel:

    - His guilt is removed
    - His sins are forgiven
    - He is fit for ministry

What caused Isaiah to fear (guilt because of sin) before God has been removed.

The Call to Ministry

> Then I heard the voice of the Lord, saying, "Whom shall I send, and who will go for Us?" Then I said, "Here am I. Send me!"
> - Isaiah 6:8

God revealed Himself to Isaiah for a reason and that was to prepare him for ministry. Notice that the word says, "Then I heard the Lord asking..."

- Until his cleansing, Isaiah heard the angels proclaiming God's holiness and his own heart's condemnation.

- But now he is privy to the voice of the Godhead as the Lord speaks to the council of angels and says, "Who will be His messenger to the people?"

This time Isaiah answers without fear and without shame, "Here I am. Send me." The assurance of forgiveness and the clarity of a guilt-free conscious are evident in Isaiah's desire to do God's will. So Isaiah's experience reveals three basic principles involved in God's call to ministry — any ministry at any time.

Call to Ministry Principles

Principle #1 – Veneration Before Activation

Isaiah was familiar with the temple (a worshipful attitude) before he was asked to do anything. The angels had six wings, four of these were used in acts of humility, only two were used for service. Jesus gave Mary's humble act of quiet learning the blessing over Martha's business in serving. First, we must humble ourselves and be devoted to worship and seeking the Lord's presence before we can be used in His service. We forget that our first and foremost responsibility is to adore God; the 1st commandment is to love God; the main activity of heaven is reverence of God.

And so, I repeat Principle #1 – Veneration before Activation. We will never hear God's calling if we don't first learn to be still and know He is God.

Principle #2 – Realization Before Visualization

You cannot serve God effectively if you don't have a true sense of yourself first. Look at the great servants of God in the Bible, their doubt and hesitation was often an acknowledgment of their true condition before God:

- Abraham saw his and Sarah's advanced age.
- Moses hesitated because of his perceived lack of "leadership skills."
- Daniel continually expressed his guilt and failings before God.
- Peter knew he was an unworthy sinner.
- Paul called himself the greatest of sinners.
- Isaiah immediately confessed his impurity and his impending doom because of it.

All of these men had three things in common:

1. They saw clearly and acknowledged their unworthiness and sinfulness. And not as false humility, but a true vision of who and what they really were like.
2. They all had a special vision or relationship with God.
3. They were all used in a mighty way in God's service.

Realization before visualization means that the more you see yourself as you really are, the more you will be able to see God as He really is (and see Him as He reveals Himself through His word). And the greater your vision of Him, the more you are able to understand and receive a call to ministry from Him. How can you accurately serve or tell others about God that you can't see if you don't even know who you are, a person you can see?

Principle #3 – Consecration Before Confirmation

There are usually three steps involved in a call to ministry: Calling/Consecration/Confirmation

1. The first step is the "calling" itself. God, in some way, calls us to some task, some area of ministry. For a few, in the Bible, the call came through a vision, dream, or some other supernatural phenomenon (Moses and the burning bush or Paul had a vision).

For most, however, it's an urging to serve in a particular way; or the recognition that we have a special ability; for others, it's a burden or need to **do** something to serve the Lord in some way. I usually tell people that if the idea, or feeling, that this is what you ought to be doing (in ministry) never leaves you, then that's a good sign of a calling.

2. The second step is consecration. Consecration refers to the preparation one goes through in order to carry out their ministry/calling. For example, several years separated Saul's call to ministry on the road to Damascus in Acts 9 and his actual departure with Barnabas on his first missionary journey in Acts 13. In the intervening years, he spent time in Tarsus; time in the desert; time traveling to Jerusalem; time teaching in Antioch. He was being consecrated, prepared, separated for his original calling which was to preach the gospel to the Gentiles.

Today the period of consecration can involve personal spiritual growth; formal ministry training as well as internship and mentoring. Some people think that as long as they feel "called" to serve, this qualifies them for ministry. Moses is a good example of what can happen when we skip this step. He felt God's call to lead his people and went out on his own to rally them only to end up killing an Egyptian and running for his life. He spent the next 40 years in the desert preparing for his ministry as God consecrated him for true leadership.

In Isaiah's case, what was needed was to prepare him to speak as a prophet of God. The purification of his lips was the consecration to ministry. In a sense, the altar also represented the gift of the Holy Spirit made possible by Christ's sacrifice now given to Isaiah empowering him to speak.

3. Isaiah is now ready for the third step in this process which is the confirmation to ministry. In Acts 13:3, we note that Paul and Barnabas were confirmed (some say ordained/commended) into their ministry by prayer and the laying on of hands of the prophets and teachers who were at Antioch. This followed the example of the Apostles who prayed and laid hands on the seven men who were confirmed/appointed as deacons to their ministry. Isaiah is ordained or appointed to his prophetic ministry by God Himself who "confirms" his role by sending him to the people with a specific message.

Summary

So let's close our study by going back to our title, Here Am I, Send Me. Each new year, churches invariably begin new programs, even consider selecting new elders or deacons, or perhaps add ministry staff. It's also a time when we recruit volunteers to help with Bible School or the Youth Group and so on and so forth. In all of this rush to get everyone involved, let's not overlook the basics concerning the call to minister in every area great and small. Let's summarize.

1. It is God who calls us through His Word, His Spirit, and His Church. In every instance, we are encouraging people to serve by and for the Lord. And, in every instance, when you feel the call, the urge to volunteer, to respond, this is God who calls you and it is to Him that you are responding — even if there is no majestic vision of heaven.

2. Consecration is not the same as confirmation. Some think that a degree in Bible from a college or preaching school is what makes you a minister. Or if you have a special skill in service or leadership you automatically qualify for ministry. No one in the church is self-appointed to ministry. God always uses the church to confirm someone to ministry. I.e. Saul had a vision, heard the Lord, met with the Apostles, but did not begin his "ministry" until the church laid hands on him and sent him to preach (Acts 13:1-3). In order to do things in a decent and orderly way, everyone who serves needs to be trained (consecrated) as well as confirmed by the leadership to their appointed tasks.

I pray that this lesson will stir your spirit so that you will reconsider your service to the Lord's church and your heart will be moved to say,

"Here Am I Lord, Send _____."
(YOUR NAME HERE)

7.
Christmas Before Christ

Isaiah 9:6-7

I'd like to look at Christ's birth from an Old Testament prophet's viewpoint. We usually look at this event, the birth of Christ, as something that happened in the past, but for many centuries the birth of the Messiah was seen as something in the future. Let's go back in time and examine what this great event meant for those who saw it as something to hope for somewhere in the future, rather than celebrate as a past event.

Background on Isaiah

The Old Testament period we will look at is the time of Isaiah the prophet who lived in the 7th century before Christ. At that time, the nation of Israel was divided into two kingdoms - North and South. The united kingdom under Saul, David, and Solomon was split in two by civil war after Solomon's death. Isaiah lived and worked in the Southern Kingdom and dwelt in the city of Jerusalem. He was from an influential family and was well educated. His name meant "God is Salvation" and he served as the preacher for the royal family throughout the reigns of several kings including Uzziah, Jotham, Ahaz, and Hezekiah. (All kings of the Southern Kingdom.)

Isaiah made many prophecies concerning what would happen to Judah, the Southern Kingdom, within a century's time, and history verifies that all of his prophecies came true. One such prophecy was given as the entire region was going through a severe crisis. Isaiah had predicted that the Northern Kingdom would be destroyed and the people taken into captivity. This took place shortly after, as Assyria came in and conquered the Northern Kingdom and scattered its people (721 BC). In addition to the prophecy about this terrible event, Isaiah made another prophecy saying that despite this region's terrible defeat, there would one day come from it a Wonderful Savior who would bestow favor on it before the world.

> [6] For a child will be born to us, a son will be given to us;
> And the government will rest on His shoulders;
> And His name will be called Wonderful Counselor, Mighty God,
> Eternal Father, Prince of Peace.
> [7] There will be no end to the increase of His government or of peace,
> On the throne of David and over his kingdom,
> To establish it and to uphold it with justice and righteousness
> From then on and forevermore.

> The zeal of the Lord of hosts will accomplish this.
> - Isaiah 9:6-7

For the people of that time, this prophecy foretold not only of destruction but of hope that a period of peace and restoration would come. The fortunes of those kingdoms went up and down throughout history:

- The Northern Kingdom was never restored and eventually became the dwelling place of a mixed-race called Samaritans who hated and were hated in return by Jews in the Southern Kingdom.
- The Southern Kingdom itself was defeated and destroyed and its people carried off into captivity to Babylon (587 BC).
- They returned 70 years later, a small remnant, to rebuild the city and temple but never regained the old glory and wealth that they had under Solomon.

All the prophecies that Isaiah made about their military and political future were fulfilled except this one concerning the child born, the Wonderful Counselor, etc. As time went by those who longed for the Messiah, spoken of by many of the prophets including Isaiah, looked to this particular prophecy to indicate the great joy experienced when the Messiah would be born.

Christmas Joy in the Old Testament

Of course, the Jews didn't celebrate Christmas in the Old Testament but the thought or anticipation of the birth of the Messiah did bring them joy (like it does for us today) for several reasons particular to them:

1. His birth would signal the end of the reign of Satan on earth - vs. 6a

The term government refers to empire and the word shoulders refers to authority. From the fall of Adam to the birth of Christ, Satan held men prisoners through their ignorance and fear of death (Hebrews 2:14-15). With the arrival of Jesus, sin would be atoned for and eternal death eliminated. Jesus would bring a new order, a new empire, a new authority on earth to displace the old authority of sin and death. In Matthew 28:18 Jesus says, "All authority in heaven and on earth has been given unto Me", this fulfills Isaiah's prophecy of the authority (government) resting on His shoulders.

The Jews saw this as the hope of being free from human oppressors only, but Isaiah's words had a much wider implication through Jesus. Another reason for their joyful anticipation of the Messiah:

2. His birth would give man the fullest revelation of God in history - vs. 6b

In the Old Testament, your name stood for who you were, it was a mark of individuality. Isaiah confers four names on this person to be born, and each one of these names is used to refer to divinity elsewhere in Scripture (Isaiah 28:29). Not just ordinary names or compliments, they refer to Divinity. Another feature of these names was that each one described a way in which the Messiah would reveal His divine nature to man. It's interesting to note that Jesus fulfilled each of these names during His ministry:

A. Wonderful Counselor (miraculous advisor)

- In John 16:29-30 - the Apostles believed in His divinity because of His teaching.

B. Mighty God (power)

- John 3:2 - Powerful signs were seen as a witness of His divinity.

C. Eternal Father

- Isn't it amazing that Isaiah refers to someone not yet born as eternal.
- It suggests that the one to be born as a human already existed even as his birth was being predicted.

- In John 14:8-9 Jesus says to Philip, "Have I been so long with you and yet you have not come to know Me.."
- It was the Father answering Philip directly, revealing Himself, as the Eternal Father, through Jesus Christ.

D. Prince of Peace

- Jesus did not come to bring peace between people.
- He said that there would be wars and rumors of wars until the end of time.
- He also said that because of Him there would be a conflict between people, between families. He came to bring a sword.
- No, the peace that He brought was between God and man, not man and man.
- Luke 2:14 is a most misquoted verse. Not peace between men, but peace among the men with whom He is pleased. They will have peace with God.
- John 16:33 He says, "..in Me you may have peace, in the world you have tribulation..."
- Through Jesus the world finds peace with God

Until the birth of Christ, then, the world did not really know God, but Isaiah prophesied that when the child would come everyone would:

- Learn the wisdom of God (Wonderful Counselor)
- See the works of God (Mighty God)
- Touch the form of God (Eternal Father)
- Receive the blessing of salvation (Prince of Peace)

Isaiah's prophecy foretold of a time when God would be seen even more clearly than through the prophets, like himself, who predicted His coming. They looked to His coming with joy because:

3. His birth would mark the time when the kingdom of heaven would be established here on earth - vs.7

The arrival of the child would be the point in history when the government of God would be established on earth and expand until the end of time - this coincides with Daniel's prophecy in Daniel 2:44. The New Testament reveals that God's government (kingdom) of which Christ is the head is not political but spiritual - and that spiritual kingdom is what Isaiah is talking about here. At the end of time, all governments, all human systems will fall and the only government, the only system that will remain in place will be the kingdom of God with Christ at its head.

Philippians 2:9 says that every knee will bow and every tongue will confess that Jesus is Mighty God, Prince of Peace, Wonderful Counselor and Eternal Father.

Until the birth of the Messiah spoken of by Isaiah, all were denied entry into the kingdom, but with His death and resurrection, Jesus opened wide the doors of the kingdom for all to enter in.

Summary

The point of this study is that there were legitimate reasons to rejoice at the birth of Christ long before any "Christmas" holiday was ever conceived or celebrated. Although the anticipation of gift-giving and receiving is pleasant and there is a spirit of benevolence that exists even in the most cold-hearted organizations at Christmas time, the true reasons for joy are not found here. The true reasons have nothing to do with money or traditions, they are quite Biblical in nature. His birth is a cause for joy because, as Isaiah puts it:

1. His birth signaled the end of the old regime of sin and death and the beginning of the new authority dealing with people through grace and love.
2. His birth opened our eyes to see God in a way that we could never see Him before.
3. His birth brought the glorious kingdom of heaven to earth and opened the door for all those who believed and are baptized to enter in.

I feel sorry for people who celebrate Christmas in ignorance of these facts. All they have to show for their Christmas are a few toys and a couple of extra pounds and plenty of debt. I do feel happy, however, to extend to you my brothers and sisters in Christ an invitation to rejoice at the birth of Christ - no matter how you choose to recognize this Biblical fact. Remember that your joy throughout the year is based on the fact that:

- You possess eternal life
- You have knowledge of the true God
- You are members of His glorious kingdom - the church

I praise God for sending His Son to be born as a man and blessing us with such rich and wonderful gifts. If you are only celebrating the season but can't celebrate the Son because you are not one of His disciples or you have been unfaithful, why not make that right by repenting and being baptized now (Acts 2:37-38) or being restored through prayer (I John 1:7-9). These actions will produce a truly Merry Christmas in your heart that will last throughout the year!

8.
The Suffering Servant

Isaiah 52:13-53:12

In this chapter I'd like us to look and marvel at an amazing passage of Scripture. It is found in the book of Isaiah and is considered to be one of the clearest descriptions and prophecies of Jesus' person and work contained in the Old Testament. This passage is commonly referred to as the "Suffering Servant" passage in Isaiah because it pictures the Messiah of Israel – not as a conquering political hero (as some of the people thought He would be) – but as one who would save His people through His own personal suffering.

It is an extraordinary passage because of its accuracy in describing the person, the purpose and the promise of God fulfilled through Jesus Christ – all foretold 700 years before His appearance. It is incredible because the information contained in this passage could not be applied historically, morally or theologically to any other religious leader in history except Jesus Christ: only He could be the Suffering Servant.

Therefore, the purpose of this study is to marvel and be amazed, as we examine this miraculous prophecy concerning Jesus, the Suffering Servant, as he is described by Isaiah the prophet.

Background on Isaiah

Isaiah lived in the 7th century before Christ. After Solomon died, the kingdom of Israel was divided into the Northern and Southern kingdoms. Each kingdom had its own leaders and prophets. Isaiah was a prophet in the Southern kingdom living in Jerusalem.

He was an educated man and came from a leading family and so he served the king's court as minister. Prophets served as religious and political advisors since their leaders sought the will of God in what they did as kings. This was often a source of conflict because many of the kings didn't want to follow the word of the prophets when they received it.

In this capacity, Isaiah lived and served through the reigns of several kings in Jerusalem.

During his lifetime, however, Isaiah saw the Northern Kingdom destroyed and the Assyrian army (which conquered the North) march right to the gates of Jerusalem itself. He had advised King Hezekiah not to surrender and prayed for the city and an angel stopped the foreign army and saved the city, a high point of his ministry.

His writings are a commentary on the things that took place in his own lifetime but he also prophesied about future events:

- The fall of the Northern Kingdom
- The rise of the Babylonian Empire 100 years before it happened.
- The decline of Egypt as a world power.
- The eventual fall of Jerusalem and its restoration under King Cyrus who wasn't even born when he made this prophecy.

Aside from his predictions, Isaiah also spoke of the spiritual condition of the nation and its role in the world. It is here where the image of the "Servant" comes in: Isaiah described the nation of Israel as God's servant who at times suffered because of its relationship to God but would one day be vindicated, one day be restored from captivity.

Sometimes, however, he described the servant as a person, a man who would come to serve God for a special purpose. In chapters 49-55, Isaiah speaks about this idea of the servant. Sometimes it is the nation, sometimes the individual. The context determines which one. In chapters 52-53, Isaiah talks about the servant as a person and what is amazing is that through his description of the Suffering Servant he gives a perfect account of Jesus' life and ministry here on earth.

One of the reasons why the Bible is reliable is because it contains fulfilled prophecy – predictions of the future accurately described and historically completed. Isaiah 52-53 contains one of the clearest examples of fulfilled prophecy. Not simply the predictions of political events in the next 50-100 years, but an accurate description of the Christ 700 years before He arrived, accurate in every way:

1. Accurately describing His person – Could not fit any other person in history.
2. Accurately describing His purpose – The heart and soul of the Christian religion, the reason for Christ's work is described.
3. Accurately describing His promise – Through Isaiah God provided the encouragement that sinners needed long before the Christ arrived.

Let's read through the text and see Jesus as the Suffering Servant.

> ^{13} Behold, My servant will prosper,
> He will be high and lifted up and greatly exalted.
> ^{14} Just as many were astonished at you,
> My people, So His appearance was marred more

> than any man
> And His form more than the sons of men.

Here Isaiah distinguishes between the idea of the nation as servant and the Messiah as servant. Even though the nation has suffered, the suffering of this individual will be great. He immediately identifies this person as a servant and as a servant who will suffer – and this is where the idea of the "suffering servant" comes from.

> [15] Thus He will sprinkle many nations,
> Kings will shut their mouths on account of Him;
> For what had not been told them they will see,
> And what they had not heard they will understand.

This verse reveals the purpose of the Messiah's ministry and that is to cleanse. The priests would sprinkle the people with the blood of the sacrifice as a way of signifying that the sacrifice covered their sins and cleansed them of moral filth. The sprinkling of nations is a reference to the idea that the sacrifice of the Messiah would accomplish this not only for the people in the physical presence of the priest but for the entire world. Even powerful men, like kings, will be amazed because God's plan for saving man (by cleansing him from sin) will finally be revealed through this servant. Romans 16:25 (the mystery Paul speaks of).

> Vs. 53:1 - Who has believed our message? And to whom has the arm of the Lord been revealed?

Here Isaiah writes as God would Himself be speaking in the first person. God is saying that despite the things that the Messiah would do, there would be disbelief. The prophecy here is that the reaction to what the servant would do would be disbelief and history confirms that despite the miracles and teaching – the Jews first, and then the world, largely disbelieved. Once started, he goes on to describe the person of the servant.

> ² For He grew up before Him like a tender shoot,
> And like a root out of parched ground;
> He has no stately form or majesty
> That we should look upon Him,
> Nor appearance that we should be attracted to Him.
> ³ He was despised and forsaken of men,
> A man of sorrows and acquainted with grief;
> And like one from whom men hide their face
> He was despised, and we did not esteem Him.

He grew like a plain plant not in a royal garden, without special care. This refers to the humble birth of Jesus, who although He was king, chose to be born in a manger, of poor people. His early years were not spent as a king, in splendor with attention paid to Him, but in obscurity, living under submission to His parents. In His later life during His public ministry, He spent much time avoiding:

- The crowds who merely wanted bread.
- The religious leaders who wanted to trap and kill Him.

His final night was spent alone in anguished prayer and His last day a long ordeal of suffering, rejection and painful death.

> [4] Surely our griefs He Himself bore,
> And our sorrows He carried;
> Yet we ourselves esteemed Him stricken,
> Smitten of God, and afflicted.
> [5] But He was pierced through for our transgressions,
> He was crushed for our iniquities;
> The chastening for our well-being fell upon Him,
> And by His scourging we are healed.
> [6] All of us like sheep have gone astray,
> Each of us has turned to his own way;
> But the Lord has caused the iniquity of us all To fall on Him.

In these three verses, Isaiah explains the purpose of Jesus' life, death and resurrection. In three short verses are contained the core of the gospel of Jesus Christ. Most of the Old Testament is written in poetic form and Isaiah is no exception. One poetic device used was to repeat the same idea in a variety of ways (Parallelism). Here Isaiah explains that the Messiah would die for the sins of men; he explains it in three ways:

1. **He would carry our sorrow -** Some would think that it was His sadness and His sins that He bore on the cross. However, the truth of the matter was that it was our suffering and our sins that we see in His cross and death, not His own.

2. **He would experience the pain** (pierced, crushed, chastened, scourged), that we should experience when God would judge and condemn us. Death and condemnation from God caused pain and the Messiah would experience that pain on behalf of each person so that when sinners came before God – they wouldn't have to.

3. **He will bring those who are lost back home again by suffering the consequences of their lostness on their behalf.** All the things that happen to those who stray away from God – the Messiah would bear so they could go home to be with Him. Jesus, the Apostles and every person who has ever tried to preach the good news of salvation has repeated this idea to his hearers – that God sent the Messiah to die for sinners, but Isaiah explained it 700 years before it happened!

> ⁷ He was oppressed and He was afflicted,
> Yet He did not open His mouth;
> Like a lamb that is led to slaughter,
> And like a sheep that is silent before its shearers,
> So He did not open His mouth.

In this verse, Isaiah returns to describe the spirit with which the Messiah would enter into this suffering: Unlike the nation of Israel which suffered because of its rebellion and did not bear its punishment willingly or without complaint. The individual servant, the Messiah, would accept His suffering without complaint or resistance. His suffering was not due for His own sins but as a command of God for the sins of others, and for this reason He bore it quietly and without resistance for to resist was to resist God and to refuse was to lose man's opportunity for salvation.

> ⁸ By oppression and judgment He was taken away;
> And as for His generation, who considered
> That He was cut off out of the land of the living
> For the transgression of my people, to whom the stroke was due?

Here is another poetic device. After describing the person and the purpose of the Servant, the author (God) asks a question of the readers. Once the Messiah was unjustly killed and taken away, who among His own generation (or people) realized that it was for their own sins this had happened, and not His own? Once again, the idea of disbelief and misunderstanding is brought up. The Jews did not believe He was the Messiah and rejected the idea that His death was for their sins. They considered Him a blasphemer and troublemaker until the end (even to this day).

> ⁹ His grave was assigned with wicked men,
> Yet He was with a rich man in His death,
> Because He had done no violence,
> Nor was there any deceit in His mouth.

Yet, the writer says that even in death He would be justified. Evil men and criminals were buried in common graves – cut-off from their people but even though He was considered this by the people, Jesus would be buried in a proper grave. We know that the Lord was removed from the cross by Nicodemus and Joseph of Arimathea, and buried in a new tomb near the place where He died – not in a common grave, (John 19:38-42). Even though He died like a criminal, He was buried ... like a just man.

In the last verses, the promise or result of the Messiah's suffering is explained. Again this is explained in different ways.

> ¹⁰ But the Lord was pleased
> To crush Him, putting Him to grief;
> If He would render Himself as a guilt offering,
> He will see His offspring,

> He will prolong His days,
> And the good pleasure of the Lord will prosper in
> His hand.

The Servant will live to see His descendants, those who will come after Him. God's will, will be done through Him (the pleasure of the Lord will prosper in His hand).

> [11] As a result of the anguish of His soul,
> He will see it and be satisfied;
> By His knowledge the Righteous One,
> My Servant, will justify the many,
> As He will bear their iniquities.

The Servant, through His suffering, will live to see the justification (forgiveness, salvation) of those who come after Him.

> [12] Therefore, I will allot Him a portion with the great,
> And He will divide the booty with the strong;
> Because He poured out Himself to death,
> And was numbered with the transgressors;
> Yet He Himself bore the sin of many,
> And interceded for the transgressors.

He will be considered great because of His work as atoning sacrifice and mediator between God and sinners.

In other words, because of His suffering, the servant will save many, will Himself live to see these and will be exalted by God.

Summary

In this passage, written 700 years before the appearance of the Messiah, Isaiah describes perfectly three things that we now know about the Christ, Jesus:

1. **His personality** – Isaiah's description of His attitude, how He was perceived and treated and how He reacted could not fit any Jewish character or any other religious leader throughout history. No one else fits this profile, except Jesus.

2. **His purpose** – The doctrine of salvation by substitutionary atonement is perfectly explained here. He clarifies why God is doing this 700 years before He does it! Not animal sacrifice, but the willing sacrifice of God's own chosen servant on behalf of sinners, this is the basis of Christianity; no other religion has this as a central feature.

3. **His promise** – The prophecy even goes beyond the time that the actual events are going to take place. In the passage, Isaiah describes the promise that God makes to the Messiah and to those who will benefit from His appearance.

- To the Messiah the promise is that death will not be able to hold Him because He is sinless. The empty grave and witness of the Apostles confirmed this – the angels are witnesses that He is at the right hand of God.

- To those who accept Him, the promise that their sins will be forgiven, and that the punishment that they would have to endure forever has fallen on Him.

As marvelous as it is, Isaiah's prophecy could at best describe what a person could look forward to, could hope for in the future. While he lived, they had only the sacrifice of animals to appease their consciences for sin (and this only reminded them of sin, it didn't cleanse their guilty consciences).

We, on the other hand, have the blessing of having seen his prophecy fulfilled and have, today, access to the sacrifice of the Messiah to wash away our sins, to guarantee our salvation and to protect us against the judgment to come. What he through the miracle of prophecy saw, we through the word of God have access to now – the opportunity to be saved through Jesus Christ.

Jesus said it Himself in Mark 16:16, "Those who believe and are baptized will be saved."

9.
The True Fast

Isaiah 58:1-14

A recent prayer and fasting weekend at church has reminded me of when I was a Catholic boy growing up in Quebec, I would give up candy during Lent. Lent was a period of 40 days between Ash Wednesday and the eve of Easter Sunday commemorating the 40 days Jesus spent in the desert fasting and praying.

People would also "fast" during this period by giving up cigarettes or meat or alcohol. After Easter, however, they would go back to their normal routine. Although there were probably good intentions here, most folks missed the point about fasting and what God required of it.

When we think of "fasting" we usually think of food and going hungry for a time. Although this may be true to an extent, the denial of food for a time is only a small part of what fasting is all about.

In chapter 58 of the book of Isaiah, the prophet explains to the Jews what God requires when they fast and what a "true" fast is all about.

In this chapter, Isaiah speaks about the Jews and their misunderstanding not only about God's requirements for a fast but also their ignorance concerning those things that really please God.

> "Cry loudly, do not hold back;
> Raise your voice like a trumpet,
> And declare to My people their transgression
> And to the house of Jacob their sins.
> - Isaiah 58:1

The chapter begins as Isaiah quotes God as He is speaking directly to His people and is telling them that they are sinners and that they need to know what their sins are.

Now, Isaiah has spoken repeatedly to them about this but they ignore him and go about their religious practices without noticing him or his words against them.

> "Yet they seek Me day by day and delight to know My ways,
> As a nation that has done righteousness
> And has not forsaken the ordinance of their God.
> They ask Me *for* just decisions,
> They delight in the nearness of God.
> - Isaiah 58:2

Despite this wickedness, God says that they continually seek Him to reward them with spiritual blessings. They act just like a people who actually obey Him. They're not just hypocrites, their clueless.

> 'Why have we fasted and You do not see?
> *Why* have we humbled ourselves and You do not notice?'
> Behold, on the day of your fast you find *your* desire,
> And drive hard all your workers.
> - Isaiah 58:3

In this verse, God mocks them by repeating their own words back to Himself as a dialogue. In the discussion they complain that they fast and yet God doesn't reward them in some way. God answers that they fast "externally" (perhaps some type of ceremonial fasting) but their inner person is not changed. The proof is that they still treat others (their slaves and workers) with contempt in the pursuit of profit.

> "Behold, you fast for contention and strife and to strike with a wicked fist.
> You do not fast like *you do* today to make your voice heard on high.
> - Isaiah 58:4

God describes the results of their so-called "fast" and tells them that it will not produce what they want. It won't reach heaven meaning that their prayers won't be heard. Their so-called fast won't produce a more spiritual person - in fact the way they perform this spiritual exercise will only increase their wickedness in God's eyes.

> "Is it a fast like this which I choose, a day for a man to humble himself?
> Is it for bowing one's head like a reed
> And for spreading out sackcloth and ashes as a bed?
> Will you call this a fast, even an acceptable day to the Lord?
> - Isaiah 58:5

God questions them on the externals that they meticulously followed in their fasting. To bow the head in prayer and humility. To dress humbly in rough garments and sprinkle ashes on the head as a sign of sorrow for sin. These externals were to represent a humble and contrite heart because of sin and failure, trial and sorrow, as in the case of Job for example. In the end these things signified a person's need for God and His salvation.

In the following verses, however, God will describe not just the ceremonial fasting that represented a contrite heart, but He will also describe those actions which proved that the fasting was sincere. He mentions three things that were directed towards the people of Isaiah's day but can also be applied to every generation of God's people who seek a true fast before the Lord. In these verses, He also describes the rewards that come with a true fast.

The first external sign of a true fast:

1. Mercy

> [6] "Is this not the fast which I choose,
> To loosen the bonds of wickedness,
> To undo the bands of the yoke,
> And to let the oppressed go free
> And break every yoke?
> [7] "Is it not to divide your bread with the hungry
> And bring the homeless poor into the house;
> When you see the naked, to cover him;
> And not to hide yourself from your own flesh?
> [8] "Then your light will break out like the dawn,
> And your recovery will speedily spring forth;
> And your righteousness will go before you;
> The glory of the Lord will be your rear guard.
> [9a] "Then you will call, and the Lord will answer;
> You will cry, and He will say, 'Here I am.'
> - Isaiah 58:6-9a

A true fast will produce Godly qualities like mercy that in Jewish Society showed itself in the freeing of those who were enslaved in one way or another. Care for those who were in physical need (the hungry and naked). The support of one's own family and other such acts of mercy and kindness which would be rewarded by the Lord.

- Mercy provides a great witness of one's faith.
- God promises to heal the sadness of the soul (depression, anxiety) mercy being an antidote to depression.
- The merciful become acceptable to God (how they share in His glory)
- And their prayers will be answered.

A true fast produces a merciful and compassionate heart which God rewards in a variety of ways.

2. A True Fast Produces Truth

> [9b] If you remove the yoke from your midst,
> The pointing of the finger and speaking wickedness,
> [10] And if you give yourself to the hungry
> And satisfy the desire of the afflicted,
> Then your light will rise in darkness
> And your gloom *will become* like midday.
> [11] "And the Lord will continually guide you,
> And satisfy your desire in scorched places,

> And give strength to your bones;
> And you will be like a watered garden,
> And like a spring of water whose waters do not fail.
> ¹² "Those from among you will rebuild the ancient ruins;
> You will raise up the age-old foundations;
> And you will be called the repairer of the breach,
> The restorer of the streets in which to dwell.
> - Isaiah 58:9b-12

A sign that one's heart is turning towards God is a greater desire to be truthful. One begins speaking with the purpose of healing and nourishing others: What's understood here is that the speaking of the truth in love - this is what nourishes a hungry soul.

The Jews hated Gentiles and anyone not in their social class or family. They were originally chosen by God to speak the "truth" to the Gentiles and live as a light to them. The Jews of Isaiah's time had failed miserably in both these responsibilities.

A true fast would see this truthful attitude towards others returning and rewarded! Speaking the truth would do several things:

- Their nation would be restored to greatness, not degraded and threatened as they were in Isaiah's day - vs. 10

- As a people, they would experience peace and joy in the Lord. vs.11
- Their generation would be remembered as the one that rebuilt the nation and returned it to faith in the Lord.

A true fast produces clarity of vision and the ability to know and tell the truth which is the first criterion for personal or national greatness.

3. A True Fast Produces Holiness

> [13] "If because of the sabbath, you turn your foot
> From doing your *own* pleasure on My holy day,
> And call the sabbath a delight, the holy *day* of the Lord honorable,
> And honor it, desisting from your *own* ways,
> From seeking your *own* pleasure
> And speaking *your own* word,
> [14] Then you will take delight in the Lord,
> And I will make you ride on the heights of the earth;
> And I will feed you *with* the heritage of Jacob your father,
> For the mouth of the Lord has spoken."
> - Isaiah 58:13-14

In that day, to truly keep the Sabbath meant that the individual sincerely gave himself over to the worship of the Lord on that day. The idea was to rest from worldly activity in order to spend it with the Lord. The Jews, however, created all kinds of loopholes to permit Sabbath-keeping but still do what they wanted to do.

And much of what they did was sinful, even on the Sabbath. A true fast, however, would produce a sincere and acceptable worship and this, in turn, would be blessed by the Lord in a variety of ways.

- They would actually benefit personally from their worship. They would truly get to know the Lord, experience Him and delight in their fellowship with Him.
- Their worship would yield the wisdom to know how to live a more Godly life (i.e. vision of the high places)
- God would feed them (satisfy them) with the promise of a savior (this was their heritage from Jacob).

A true fast draws one nearer to God and from that fellowship comes the taste of eternal life with God and the courage to live faithfully until that time comes. If we were to read on we would see that despite this admonition to offer God a true and sincere fast, the Jews continued their hypocrisy and were eventually crushed and taken into captivity by the Babylonian army.

Summary

Although it was written centuries ago to a people whose culture and history are very different than ours, Isaiah's admonition fits our modern situation today. In many ways we play the same game with our religion while God waits for us to offer Him a true fast so He can bless us. By "game" I mean that we play at church, going through the motions as Christians, but God still requires proof of inward change:

He still wants to see:

1. **Mercy** - Is our faith making us more merciful? Are we more forgiving, more tolerant, more willing to not take offense? Has anyone been on the receiving end of our mercy lately? Unfortunately, half the work in the church is calming people down because they're upset or offended at something someone said or did. They're ready to quit the church even quit the Lord because they've had their feathers ruffled. A little more time focused on the cross and a little less on our feelings would cultivate mercy in one's heart.

2. **Truth** - I've calculated that in the last ten years I've preached hundreds of sermons and over a thousand bible classes on various subjects. I'm thinking that by now, most of us should know the truth - we've certainly been taught it. The question is, has anyone heard or seen the truth coming from you? Knowing it

is not enough, demonstrating and sharing it is what pleases the Lord.

3. **Holiness -** Is our religion some clean suit or dress we put on for church service and then leave in the closet for work? The Jews were the light to the Gentiles, in the same way, Jesus says we are the light of the world. The question is, "Has our religious experience led us to be lights at work, school or other places? If it hasn't, then either our religion is wrong or we're not practicing it correctly. I once taught a class at Great Lakes Christian Bible College on preaching. One of the points I made to the students is that eventually, you have to get to the point!

Because some ministers preach and preach but never get to it, I don't want to make this mistake so here's the point of this lesson.

Let's not forget what our religion is about.

The "true fast" that Isaiah talked about was the sincere expression of religion - not just the externals. Religious people, then and now, have to always be careful to remember what their religion is about.

In Isaiah's book God reminded the Jews, and by extension reminds us that our religion is about:

1. **Mercy -** Our showing mercy to others in big and little ways - just as Christ shows us mercy in big and little ways.

2. **Truth -** Our sharing the truth with those outside the church building, not just hearing the truth preached to us twice a week. The preacher's task is to teach the church so the church can teach others, not so that the members can judge how good or enjoyable his lessons are.

3. **Holiness -** God wants us to be holy, not just act holy during worship services. If you don't like being holy (meaning pure, good, sincere) then you won't like heaven because there's no sin there - only holiness.

To be a religious person you must not be ashamed of your holiness because that's what separates you from the world. Some Christians are embarrassed by their holiness because they still want to be accepted by the world.

You can't have it both ways, either you belong to Christ or you don't. You can fool the world, you can fool the church but you can't fool the Lord who will judge you.

As I close this chapter I want each person reading this book (young or old; new Christian or experienced saint) to ask yourself if this lesson is truly for you. I know that it isn't for everyone because there are many who know what a true fast is, they understand what Christianity is all about and are living their lives in a pleasing way before the Lord - and being blessed for it:

- They have a peaceful heart.
- They possess a joyful attitude and hope for the future.
- They enjoy fruitful service.

But, on the other hand, if this lesson is speaking to you and challenging your ways, don't be like the Jews who heard Isaiah's message but ignored its call for change.

- Do something to respond to God's admonition.
- Get on your knees at home and call on Him for help.
- Begin living your life in the way you know God wants you to live it.

Let's make sure our religion is not just on the outside; let's be absolutely sure that it's on the inside as well.

Then and only then will it really make its way to the outside of our character and out into the community and the world where it will glorify God and Christ.

Made in the USA
Columbia, SC
09 June 2022